THE DUBS
THE ROAD TO SAM MAGUIRE

Words by **MALACHY CLERKIN**
Photographs by **INPHO**

PENGUIN
IRELAND

PENGUIN IRELAND

Published by the Penguin Group
Penguin Ireland, 25 St Stephen's Green, Dublin 2, Ireland
(a division of Penguin Books Ltd)
Penguin Books Ltd, 80 Strand, London WC2R 0RL, England
Penguin Group (USA) Inc., 375 Hudson Street, New York, New York 10014, USA
Penguin Group (Australia), 250 Camberwell Road,
Camberwell, Victoria 3124, Australia (a division of Pearson Australia Group Pty Ltd)
Penguin Group (Canada), 90 Eglinton Avenue East, Suite 700, Toronto, Ontario, Canada M4P 2Y3
(a division of Pearson Penguin Canada Inc.)
Penguin Books India Pvt Ltd, 11 Community Centre,
Panchsheel Park, New Delhi – 110 017, India
Penguin Group (NZ), 67 Apollo Drive, Rosedale, Auckland 0632, New Zealand
(a division of Pearson New Zealand Ltd)
Penguin Books (South Africa) (Pty) Ltd, 24 Sturdee Avenue,
Rosebank, Johannesburg 2196, South Africa
Penguin Books Ltd, Registered Offices: 80 Strand, London WC2R 0RL, England

www.penguin.com

First published 2011
1

Designed by Smith & Gilmour, London
Printed in Germany by Mohn media

A CIP catalogue record for this book is available from the British Library

ISBN: 978-1-844-88289-2

Photo credits:
Ryan Byrne: 36, 39 (bottom), 48–9, 53 (both), 67, 69, 106, 107, 108–9, 120, 132, 144, 146, 150, 151 (both).
James Crombie: 26, 27, 44, 54, 55, 58–9, 102, 105, 110, 112, 113, 114, 116–17, 128–9, 130, 131, 136, 140, 141,
142, 143, 152–3, 158, 164, 172, 174 (bottom), 174–5, 190, 196, 198–9, 206 (both), 210, 211, 212, 214.
Donall Farmer: 6, 12, 19, 20, 23, 24–5, 28 (top), 30, 34, 39 (top), 40, 42, 43, 62, 64, 68, 70–71, 73 (both),
74, 76–7, 122, 123, 124–5, 134, 135, 137, 138, 148, 155 (both), 156–7, 159, 184, 186–7, 188–9, 192, 215,
216–17, 218, 219, 220–21, 222 (top).
Tom Honan: 14.
Cathal Noonan: 1, 2–3, 10–11, 18, 50–51, 57, 60, 75, 78, 84–5, 88–9, 96, 115, 160, 162–3, 165, 167, 174 (top),
194, 195, 197, 202, 210, 211, 213, 222 (bottom), 223 (both).
Colm O'Neill: 93 (bottom), 94–5, 97.
Lorraine O'Sullivan: 41, 126.
Andrew Paton: 17.
Billy Stickland: 28 (bottom).
Morgan Treacy: 15, 37, 80, 82, 86, 90–91, 93 (top), 98–9, 166, 168–9, 171 (both), 180 (both), 181, 193,
200–201, 204, 207, 208–9, 224.

CONTENTS

PROLOGUE
ONE KICK

When it's your day of days, even the fixtures and fittings look like decorations. Diarmuid Connolly turned away from Aidan O'Mahony underneath the Cusack Stand, lost for an option beyond a meat-and-drink handpass inside to Kevin McManamon. His fisted pass looped a little in the air and actually overshot McManamon's run ever so slightly.

As a result of it being a touch overhit, McManamon had to lurch to the left to grab the ball, which put his body in the perfect angle to pivot quickly to the right as he ran onto it. Had Connolly's pass been flat and into McManamon's chest, he would have run straight into Barry John Keane and either been done for charging or possibly gobbled up in the tackle. But his rapid left-right soft-shoe shuffle threw the young Kerry substitute.

No sooner had referee Joe McQuillan's whistle sounded than Bernard Brogan had made up his mind what was going to happen next. Watch the replay again sometime and when the TV pictures show the second angle – from a camera in the Cusack Stand – you can see that McManamon has only just finished sprawling on the turf when Brogan waves his hand in the air to beckon Stephen Cluxton forward from the Canal End goal.

OPPOSITE
Referee Joe McQuillan encourages Stephen Cluxton to hurry up and take his free while Bernard Brogan looks on.

No sooner had referee Joe McQuillan's whistle sounded than Bernard Brogan had made up his mind what was going to happen next.

Think about that. Brogan was the reigning Footballer of the Year. He'd already kicked four frees of his own in the game. True, this wasn't on his preferred side but he'd scored points from that exact spot on the pitch numerous times in his career, numerous times in the previous few months in fact. Yet his reaction to McQuillan's whistle was instant. The thought of grabbing the glory for himself never entered his head, not even for a split second.

This was Pat Gilroy's Dublin, where everything was dreamed up anew in some shape or form. When the manager took over three years beforehand, Connolly would have been just as likely to try an impossible shot at the posts over his shoulder in that scenario, rather than make the pass. Back then, too, McManamon was hardly anyone's idea of a game-changer, yet here he was shaping the final just as he'd shaped the semi-final against Donegal. And yeah, chances are Bernard Brogan would have fancied a crack at kicking the game-winning free. He'd have taken a good look at the posts anyway.

But this one was Cluxton's and maybe the oddest thing about it was that nobody thought it odd. All year, he'd redefined what goalkeeping can be in Gaelic football. His pure striking of the dead ball off hardly any run-up had dictated much of Dublin's play from his kick-outs and he'd done his bit up the other end of the pitch as well. He was already Dublin's fourth highest scorer of the summer after the Brogan brothers and Connolly. A goalkeeper the best man to kick a free to win the All Ireland? The utter simplicity of it made you ponder why it had never happened before.

Then again, not every goalkeeper is a Stephen Cluxton. In the Dublin squad, he had long been considered the alpha and omega of trainers. First there, last to leave. He'd have been the one who put the figs in the Fig Rolls if that's what the session had called for.

Back in January, the *Irish Independent* had sent a reporter and a photographer out to Clontarf to watch the Dublin squad train at 6.30 in the morning. Even then, even in the dead black nothing of a frozen winter pre-dawn, Cluxton was the first player out of the dressing room,

This was Pat Gilroy's Dublin, where everything was dreamed up anew in some shape or form.

As Cluxton walked up the pitch in front of the 82,300 full house at Croke Park, it was easy to imagine him thinking of the hundreds of kicking sessions he'd put in over the years.

at 6.17. The city was asleep in warm beds for miles in every direction while the Dubs toiled to put a little of September's heat into their bones, and nobody welcomed the suffering more readily than the goalkeeper.

As Cluxton walked up the pitch in front of the 82,300 full house at Croke Park, it was easy to imagine him thinking of the hundreds of kicking sessions he'd put in over the years. Or the amount of abuse he'd taken from the crowds behind his various goals when a short kick-out hadn't come off. Or worse, when one had been returned for a score. It was easy to imagine him pondering any number of things in this vein because he was taking his own sweet time about trotting up the pitch.

When McQuillan had blown his whistle for the foul on McManamon, the clock had read 70:51. There were only to be two minutes of added time to be played and so the last thing Cluxton wanted to do was rush the kick and give Kerry a shot at another attack. McQuillan saw him dragging his feet and waved him forward. Cluxton didn't want to risk the referee losing patience and hopping the ball, so he broke into a jog.

He placed the ball and took five steps backwards and two to his right. As he began his run-up, the clock read 71:50. This was it, this was the season. After his kick, there would be time for nothing else. After a decade and a half of pain for the Dubs, this was one kick to end it all, one kick to win it all.

THE WILDERNESS YEARS

CHAPTERONE

Dessie Farrell tells a great story in his autobiography about the day after Dublin won their twenty-second All Ireland senior football title in 1995. They'd had their civic reception in College Green in front of 20,000 people and had done the open-topped bus routine up O'Connell Street as well. It was evening now and they were a tired bunch, empty from the effort and from its aftermath too.

The day before, Keith Barr had told RTÉ it was great to finally get the donkey off their backs. In the circumstances – after having won four Leinster titles in a row and only now converting one into an All Ireland – it felt like a curiously apt phrase. A first All Ireland in twelve years and a first for a team of men who been through the ringer in search of one. Yeah, donkey off their backs sounded about right.

When they got to the top of O'Connell Street and past the crowds, their official duties were done for the day. It was time now for families and friends and letting go. As the bus rounded Parnell Square and turned on to Gardiner Street to leave them all back to their cars, they were alone with their thoughts for the first time since the final whistle the previous day. There were no throngs left, nobody on the street looking for a piece of them.

In fact, the only person they could see out of the window of the bus as they stopped at a set of traffic lights was a little kid on a BMX. The boy looked up at the bus and saw them all in their shirts and ties, then headed off about his business. He rode halfway down the street before pulling the brakes and turning back to come up beside the bus again, as it was still stopped at the lights.

And looking up again at all these newly-minted heroes of the city, these bringers of joy, these weavers of dreams, the little kid on his BMX delivered his verdict. 'Yiz fuckin' gobshites!' he shouted before racing away into the inner-city dusk.

ABOVE
Paul Curran and
John O'Leary lift the
Sam Maguire Cup
after Dublin's All
Ireland win in 1995.

They were far from that. They were All Ireland champions, and they – and their fans – would have expected more glory to follow. This didn't look like a crew of old-timers nabbing an All Ireland just before they walked out the door. John O'Leary, Charlie Redmond and Paul Clarke were the oldest members of the squad, but they still had a few years left in them yet. There was a core of men in their mid to late twenties as well, the likes of Farrell and Barr, Mick Galvin and Brian Stynes.

And then there was the new breed, led by Paul Curran and Jason Sherlock and soon to be joined by a leggy youngster from Raheny named Ciarán Whelan and a 20-year-old defender from the Ballymun Road called Paddy Christie, who had actually been on the panel for the league that year but had missed the summer with a broken finger. With very few really exceptional teams around just then, there would surely be another All Ireland in this Dublin squad in reasonably short order.

This didn't look like a crew of old-timers nabbing an All Ireland just before they walked out the door.

There were a million reasons Dublin would go a decade and a half without even an All Ireland final appearance.

Momentum can become a runaway train. That's fine if you catch hold of it and go along for the ride, but it can leave you choking in the dust if you don't. Shortly before the start of the 1995–96 league campaign, Dr Pat O'Neill walked away from the job of Dublin manager. Although O'Neill had always intended leaving at the end of the 1995 championship to return full-time to his medical practice, most folk just assumed Sam Maguire would make a convincing enough case for him to stay on. Most folk were wrong.

It would be going overboard to blame what followed on this one thing, ludicrous to think that simple regime change was the cause of the 16 years of abyss that followed. It's akin to holding a new government in a sub-Saharan nation wholly responsible when famine strikes. There were a million reasons Dublin would go a decade and a half without even an All Ireland final appearance – big-picture stuff like the success of the peace process in the North and the rise of rugby played its part, as did tiny things like the width of a post in front of Hill 16.

OPPOSITE
Ray Cosgrove shows
his disappointment
at hitting the post
with a kick that
would have forced
a replay against
Armagh in 2002.

But when fire investigators go into a smouldering house, they use the flame-damage only as a clue to help them work backwards. Eventually they find the origin of the fire, the point at which things went from being calm and normal and everyday to being anything but. Dublin football history changed when the management changed in the wake of the '95 All Ireland. The momentum was lost and with it went the goodwill and the sense of progress. Without these things, a playing squad will only achieve so much.

In slicing up the blame pie, everybody is entitled to their portion. Mickey Whelan was probably the right man at the wrong time in the autumn of 1995. An All Ireland winner on the pitch and a fine coach off it, he came upon a squad of grown men and decided to treat them as such. When training was occasionally slack that winter, he wasn't often inclined to take some of them by the ear. They hadn't been beaten in Leinster since the four-match epic against Meath in 1991 and had just lifted Sam. There may have seemed little to be gained in scolding them for cutting a few corners at training.

The players, too, earned their share of blame. They weren't all sated by reaching the promised land, but it's undeniable that some of them were. Human nature, nothing more and nothing less. Farrell heard one or two say in the aftermath of the All Ireland that they didn't care if they never won another match. That kind of thing seeps in like winter rain.

By the time Meath got a hold of them in the 1996 Leinster final, they hadn't the same vim as in other years. They lost by 0–10 to 0–8 and just like that, their spell over the Leinster Championship was broken. It would be a full six years before they'd pick up their next one.

Whelan was unlucky to have taken over a thankless job at the worst possible time. When the only way is down, it's no fun being the pilot. That said, his reign was stormier than it needed to be and falling out with his captain John O'Leary helped nobody's cause. In what was to become a familiar theme, plenty of dirty laundry got aired in public and a soap-operatic tone was set for the next few years.

Farrell heard one or two say in the aftermath of the All Ireland that they didn't care if they never won another match.

Meath hunted them out of Leinster in the first round in '97, and league defeat to Offaly later that year sealed Whelan's fate. 'Nobody died,' he told reporters afterwards. It rang a small note of perspective amid an increasingly fraught cacophony.

Tommy Carr came in that winter and stayed for four terms, none of them particularly successful, none of them particularly lucky either. He had much to deal with, including the general rising of standards in Leinster that saw Meath (twice) and Kildare reach All Ireland finals in three out of his four years in charge. Not to mention an explosion in media attention that left no internal spat too small for a back-page splash.

Year by year, Dublin was little more than a bushfire to be extinguished without needing to send too many units to the scene. Kildare zapped them after a replay in 1998, Meath wiped them out in a Leinster final in 1999 that was more comfortable than even the five-point margin at the end suggested. Maybe 2000 was the worst of all – a seven-point thrashing in the Leinster final replay against Kildare after going in at half-time six points ahead.

It was an era of one step forward and two steps back. It felt like every new player they unearthed, from Wayne McCarthy to Colin Moran, was hailed as a saviour, and every early win in Leinster was held up as evidence that the good times were about to roll again. A perfect example was 2001, when they put 2–19 on Longford and then fought through a tight one against Offaly to make the final.

But Meath lay in wait again and after Graham Geraghty sneaked in for a very soft goal early on, Dublin were basically held at arm's length for the rest of the day. The season ended in Thurles against Kerry after they were Maurice Fitzed out of a quarter-final win the first day and blown away by Johnny Crowley in the replay. Six weeks later Carr was gone.

By now, most people knew what they thought of Dublin. Far from the worst side in the country, a fair distance from the best. The advent of the All Ireland qualifiers meant that new and exotic match-ups were being drawn from glass bowls in high summer and some counties were

It was a measure of where Dublin were at that an up-and-comer like Sligo in 2001 or Derry in 2003 would have quite fancied the tie.

starting to meet each other in the championship for the first time in the history of the GAA. It was a measure of where Dublin were at that an up-and-comer like Sligo in 2001 or Derry in 2003 would have quite fancied the tie. Equally, it was a fair reflection of Dublin's status that they swept both sides out the gate before going on to fall to serious teams in Kerry and Armagh afterwards.

Tommy Lyons followed Carr into the big job and he at least won a title: in 2002, Dublin lifted their first Leinster crown since 1995. They did this one the hard way, conquering both Meath and Kildare en route. The newest hero of the Hill was Ray Cosgrove, a rakish full-forward from Kilmacud Crokes who stuck two goals past Meath and went on to score another three against Donegal in the All Ireland quarter-final and its replay.

Of all the years that passed between 1995 and 2011, probably none epitomized what was so thrilling and yet so frustrating about Dublin better than 2002. Lyons made them puff out their chests again and encouraged them to swagger a little like the best city teams had always done. They rolled through Leinster like it was the most natural thing in the world and, having let Donegal off the hook the first day out, they filleted them in the replay.

That was the thrilling bit. The frustrating bit came after the final whistle that day when, despite only having qualified for an All Ireland semi-final, some of the Dublin team went on a lap of honour around Croke Park. Sitting in the stand, the Armagh captain Kieran McGeeney smiled inwardly. The Dubs were giving it loads over a replay win over Donegal, a team Armagh had beaten handily in the Ulster final a few weeks earlier and in fact hadn't lost to in almost a decade.

The semi-final on 1 September was an epic, played out under a blazing back-to-school sun. Armagh took charge early on but Dublin rallied in the second half and Ciarán Whelan scored one of his booming, bring-the-house-down goals to keep them in touch. As time ran dead, Cosgrove had a free to draw the teams level and force a replay but his luck – and Dublin's – went missing. His kick came back off the post and Armagh were through to the final, where they won their first ever All Ireland.

Lyons made them puff out their chests again and encouraged them to swagger a little.

From then on, most years followed a similar pattern. Dublin would give somebody a hiding early on, would subsequently hit a speedbump along the way, would briefly raise the city's hope with an act of defiance before exiting the championship at the sight of the first serious contender they met. In 2003, they atomized Louth, lost to Laois, tonked Derry and said goodbye when they met Armagh again. In '04, they got their crisis in early when Westmeath torpedoed them out of Leinster, then strolled through the qualifiers past London, Leitrim, Longford and Roscommon before the bandwagon was derailed by Kerry in the All Ireland quarter-final.

Paul Caffrey took over from Lyons then, but though the management changed, the routine didn't shift a whole lot. They won Leinster in '05 but found Tyrone a step too far, again in the All Ireland quarter-final. In '06, they waltzed through Leinster again, only to cough up another barn-burner of a semi-final, this time to Mayo.

By now, another new wave had played their way into the set-up. Only Sherlock remained from the 1995 team, with '96 recruit Whelan still hanging in there too. They were surrounded by young colts making names for themselves. Alan Brogan and Barry Cahill, Bryan Cullen and Stephen Cluxton. Conal Keaney and Shane Ryan were there too, albeit only on a few seasons' loan from the hurling world.

At times, it felt cruel to subject them to the kind of horror that seemed to be routinely visited upon Dublin footballers. They got lots of fame but little glory. They were Dublin so they were supposed to be there or thereabouts each year. No excuses allowed or entertained.

The reality was that they were always just a tier below the highest level, and for the most part that level was pretty high. While they beavered away trying to reach an All Ireland final, Mickey Harte

While they beavered away trying to reach an All Ireland final, Mickey Harte and Jack O'Connor were putting together two of the very best teams of any era.

and Jack O'Connor were putting together two of the very best teams of any era in Tyrone and Kerry. People can talk about the Beatles and the Stones, but the Kinks weren't a bad band at all. They just didn't hit paydirt in the same way.

Put it like this – between 2002 and 2010, Dublin went out of the championship to the eventual All Ireland champions seven times, and the other two times, they went out to the eventual runners-up. With the exception of 2006 and Mayo, they rarely went out to a team they ought to have beaten. Sometimes the planets just refuse to align.

Under Caffrey they got back in the groove of gathering up Leinster titles again, but it was thin gruel by now. They swatted Laois aside in '07 and squashed a Kildare rebellion in '08. But the years always ended in the same way, shot down in a blaze of glory by players who knew what it was to win an All Ireland and would know again just a few weeks later.

By the time Pat Gilroy took over at the fag end of 2008, there was a general acceptance that things had to change. On the pitch and off it as well. Dublin's style of play meant they nearly always featured in the game of the summer, but it also meant they nearly always lost it too. The first thing Gilroy did on a training week in La Manga in January 2009 was show his new players a video of the Tyrone defeat the previous summer, pointing out all the space Tyrone's midfield and half-forwards had to

OVERLEAF
The team's custom of greeting their fans on Hill 16 caused a kerfuffle before the 2006 All Ireland semi-final, when Mayo were warming up at that end of Croke Park.

spray good ball into the inside forward line. That was going to become unacceptable under his regime.

There were new faces to come in, old faces to be let go. The sting was to be taken out of the annual hype machine that surrounded the Dublin football team, so corporate gigs for some of the better-known names were quietly but firmly frowned upon. Team-announcement press conferences took place first thing in the morning so Gilroy could get on with his day. The energy around the set-up was completely different from the beginning.

Not that it changed a whole lot in terms of results, at least initially. If anything, Dublin seemed to go backwards in Gilroy's first year. Leinster was squirrelled away without a whole lot of drama but then Dublin were torn limb from limb by Kerry in the quarter-final. Colm Cooper scored a goal after 32 seconds and Kerry won by 1–24 to 1–7 in the end. With the quote of the year, Gilroy said his men looked 'like startled earwigs' in the face of the onslaught.

Gilroy's Dublin looked different from what had gone before, they sounded different and they acted different. But nobody was overly convinced yet that they actually were any different. When 2010 saw them kicked unceremoniously out of Leinster by a rampant Meath

There had been false dawns before, of course, but none built on foundations as solid as these.

OPPOSITE TOP
Ciarán Whelan shaking hands with Kerry's Tommy Griffin after the 2009 quarter-final, which was Whelan's last match.

OPPOSITE BOTTOM
So close: the scores were level with less than 30 seconds on the clock in the 2010 All Ireland semi-final, but Cork's Donncha O'Connor slotted his free and Dublin were kept waiting another year.

side who plundered five goals, it was hard to escape the feeling that pitchforks and torches might not be far behind. They inched their way through the qualifiers, but that was what was expected of them. It seemed like years since they'd caused a shock of their own.

But then came Tyrone in the quarter-final. Harte's team might not have been the all-consuming fire of the previous years but that didn't mean dousing them felt any less meaningful for Dublin. Eoghan O'Gara's goal five minutes from the end put them into the semi-final against Cork, but it did far more than that.

O'Gara's goal was the moment when everything changed. Just like that, the energy around Dublin football was turned on its head. This was a triumph that hadn't come easily and hadn't been expected, and thus it somehow felt more real. Over the course of a decade and a half, overbearing triumphalism had given way to weary fatalism. Neither emotion was healthy.

Even though Cork pipped them in the semi-final, the bad old days seemed to be over. There had been false dawns before, of course, but none built on foundations as solid as these. Now they had a team that had made its way in the world on the back of hard work and hammer blows. There was nothing glamorous about them, nothing flash. Alan Brogan's younger brother Bernard was the nearest thing they had to a matinee idol, but Gilroy had knocked the corners off him and he'd won footballer of the year even while doing his share of the tracking back. Imagine.

Nobody fretted too much over losing to Cork, for the simple reason that few people believed the Dubs were ready to win an All Ireland in 2010. Cork were. Everyone could see that.

But 2011? Well, that was a different story. If Dublin weren't going to be ready then, they might never be. As the New Year broke with the heaviest snow in a generation, there was a gentle optimism for what the thaw might bring.

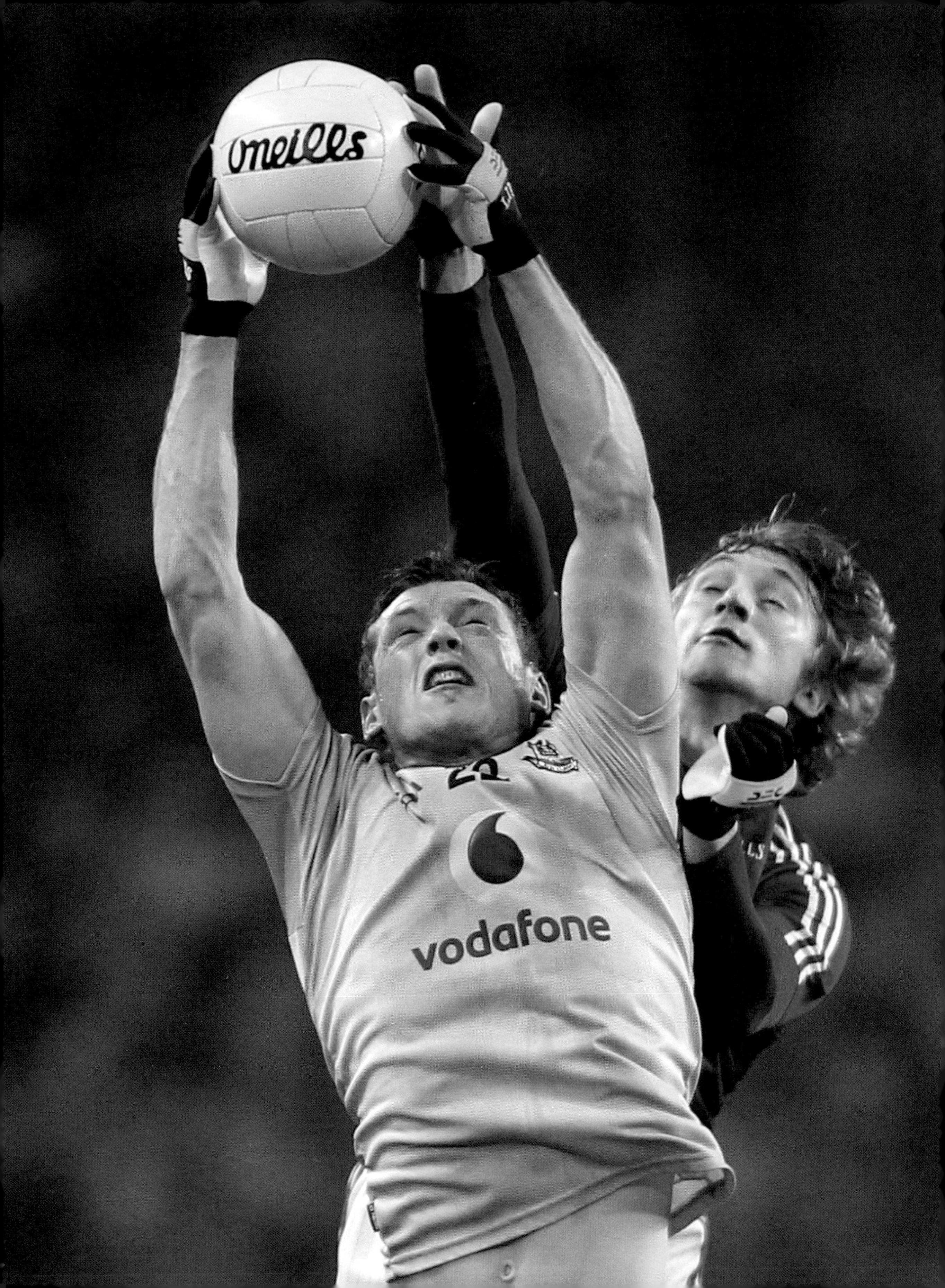
O'neills
vodafone

CHAPTER TWO
SPRINGTIME

The year coughed and wheezed into life like an old banger that been kept in the garage for too long. Pat Gilroy took his side to Mullingar for an O'Byrne Cup match against Westmeath early in January, only to find an iced-over pitch and a referee sadly shaking his head. If that was irritating for them, it was worse for the few dozen supporters who made the trip having been assured the game would go ahead, only to reach the ground as the team bus was pulling out to head back to the capital. The summer couldn't have felt further away.

No matter. Hibernation was nearly done. Westmeath actually edged the refixed game a few nights later and Gilroy turned his thoughts towards the league. This year was going to be different, on and off the pitch. The Dublin County Board had hit upon a marketing bonanza with the idea of the Spring Series, the centrepiece of which was the playing of all of Dublin's home league games at Croke Park.

It was a notion they'd been kicking around for a few seasons, but they'd never been able to do it the way they wanted. 'The last number of years, Croke Park would not have been available,' said Dublin CEO John Costello. 'Due to the scheduling of the IRFU and FAI fixtures it wasn't possible, as we didn't want Croke Park for just one particular night. We decided we wanted to play all of the games there and this year it's worked out.'

The plan was bigger than just playing a few matches at HQ. There would be double-headers with the county's hurlers where possible, half-time entertainment in the form of Jedward, Damien Dempsey and Horslips. Above all, ticket prices would be kept to a minimum – €45 for all four matches, €35 if you wanted to stand on the Hill. A parent and child could go to all four for €55. 'Dublin can command figures of

OPPOSITE
Dublin lost to
Westmeath in the
first round of the
O'Byrne Cup on
a filthy night in
Mullingar.

60,000-plus attending our matches during the summer,' said Costello. 'Reaching out to those people is the idea behind this. And to become more commercial.'

The tills rang, the stiles turned. By the end of the campaign, the Spring Series had brought over 110,000 people through the gates for Dublin's four home matches in the league. There was a brief outbreak of antler-butting between the Dublin County Board and the GAA at one point when a proposal to play the Mayo game on the Friday night after St Patrick's Day was cold-shouldered by the authorities, but otherwise everyone was sweet. Everyone in Dublin, anyway.

Inside the whitewash, Gilroy's team was coming together brick by brick. With Kilmacud Crokes still keeping a finger in the club championship pie until late February, Gilroy went into the league without three of his first-choice defence in Cian O'Sullivan, Rory O'Carroll and Kevin Nolan. Gilroy, unperturbed, just used it as an excuse to see who else he could find to depend on. New names and old names alike were given a chance. In came James McCarthy and Seán Murray, Alan Hubbard and Paul Brogan. The league would kick their tyres, see if they were roadworthy.

In attack, Gilroy had lost Niall Corkery over the winter. A strong-running, diligent wing-forward who was a photofit of the kind of player the manager needed for the game he wanted to play, the 26-year-old Corkery had moved to London to work in the financial sector. There was a spot there up for grabs and both Paul Flynn and Kevin McManamon got a run in the side in search of it. Eoghan O'Gara and Mossy Quinn were handed game time too.

Dublin and the league had been uneasy bedfellows for most of the previous decade. Often, the depression that had followed another devastating championship exit had been hard to shake off come springtime, and they just hadn't been able to get themselves up for it in any meaningful way. They were always good for a whizz-bang

By the end of the campaign, the Spring Series had brought over 110,000 people through the gates for Dublin's four home matches in the league.

OPPOSITE
Pat Gilroy with Conor
Counihan, manager of
defending All Ireland
champions Cork,
before the league
clash in February.

performance or two in each campaign but were equally reliable for
the occasional careless whimper too.

Gilroy wanted more out of the competition. The notion that
Dublin were successful enough to be blasé about it didn't sit right
with him. The way he saw it, he only had his team for maybe a dozen
competitive games in a year, with possibly a couple more thrown in if
their championship extended into August. Shrugging their shoulders
at a few league matches made no sense. They hadn't won it since 1993,
hadn't been in a final since 1999. Even if only for the sake of novelty,
they ought to set about making some sort of shape at it.

They'd only been finding their feet in the 2009 campaign, but Gilroy's
second one had gone a lot better, with only their head-to-head record
against Cork keeping them out of the final. In 2011, they were ready,
willing and able.

Armagh were up first. Or, to put a finer point on it, Dublin were up
in Armagh first on the opening Saturday night. They came away with
a 2–12 to 1–11 win against Paddy O'Rourke's newly-promoted side,
a palmed Bernard Brogan goal in the last 10 minutes putting clear water
between the teams just at the right time. O'Gara and Diarmuid Connolly
had put in a reasonable hour apiece and Gilroy came back south content
with what he'd seen.

Cork and Kerry came to Croke Park for the first two games of the
Spring Series and were both sent home with a flea in their ear. Cork
actually took a bit of a pasting on a night when Bernard Brogan was
delighting in being the brains of the operation, setting up goals for
Quinn, McManamon and Barry Cahill. And against Kerry, they ran
in another three goals – again from Quinn and McManamon with
Michael Darragh Macauley joining in this time – but came out just
the solitary point ahead.

Cork and Kerry came to Croke Park for the first two games of the Spring Series and were both sent home with a flea in their ear.

'Goals are saving our bacon in these games,' said Gilroy after the Kerry game, which was the second in a row in which Dublin had conceded 16 scores. 'We must have the worst defensive record in the league so we have a lot of work to do.'

For all his attempts to keep a lid on things, Gilroy's Dublin were making undeniably promising noises. They had beaten the All Ireland champions from the previous two years on successive Saturday nights in Croke Park in front of decent crowds. This was all good, nourishing stuff.

And they were digging out players as they went. James McCarthy was cementing a place for himself at wing-back. Lean and tall and strong, he wasn't averse to the occasional sally forward and had stitched a point against Cork into the bargain. McManamon was

'We must have the worst defensive record in the league so we have a lot of work to do.'

OPPOSITE TOP
Stephen Cluxton
and Colm Cooper
contest a high
ball in the box.

OPPOSITE BOTTOM
Kevin McManamon
emerged during the
league campaign as
a forward who knew
how to cause havoc
in defences.

growing in confidence at centre half-forward and his doughty running style had caused problem for each of Dublin's opponents. His goal against Kerry would carry echoes later in the year too, a neat sidestep taking him into space before he finished to the net. Few players in the country seemed so set on running at defenders and getting them turned around.

Wins over Monaghan, Mayo and Down kept the show rolling and nailed a spot in the final. By now, the team Gilroy would send out to play in the championship was taking shape. When they played Galway in the last game before the final, their front six were Flynn, Pat Burke, Bryan Cullen, Alan Brogan, Connolly, Bernard Brogan. With the exception of Burke, all of them would start every game they for which they were available until year's end.

Crucially, though, Alan Brogan wasn't available for the final after he was sent off seven minutes into the Galway match for an off-the-ball tussle with Johnny Duane. Coupled with the eight-week suspension O'Gara had picked up for an altercation with Marc Ó Sé at the end of the Kerry game, it meant that Dublin were going into the league final short of two of their most explosive grenades.

For much of the league final, it looked as though Dublin would barely notice their absences. Bernard Brogan was having one of those just-give-me-the-ball days where every touch he had seemed to draw a gasp. He put Mossy Quinn in for an early goal, and although Cork reeled Dublin in by the twentieth minute, it was Brogan who immediately put them ahead again.

Three minutes into the second half, he had a goal of his own to show for the torrid day he'd been giving Michael Shields, the All Star full-back in each of the last two years. And when Connolly lobbed over a point soon after, it put Dublin 2–12 to 0–10 ahead. A first league title in 18 years was half an hour away – they had the game in the bag, they only had to tie the knot in it.

But it wasn't to be. Inch by inch and point by point, Cork tapped them on the shoulder and reminded them there was a game still to

Inch by inch and point by point, Cork tapped them on the shoulder and reminded them there was a game still to be played.

be played. Cullen went off injured on 47 minutes, Bernard Brogan and Connolly soon after. It meant that when Cork scored four points in as many minutes to wipe out their lead eight minutes from time, Dublin had nobody to turn to who could grab the lead back. Dean Kelly blazed wide when straight through on goal, Quinn missed a handy free. Four minutes later, the young Cork forward Ciarán Sheehan cut in from the right and popped the winning score with his left foot. Dublin ended the game with two points in the closing 30 minutes.

The charitable view was that this wasn't a disgrace. Cork were reigning All Ireland and league champions. They had been around the block and had fallen on their faces just as many times as Dublin had. The difference was they knew what it was like to win, they knew the value of patience.

The less charitable view was that this was nothing new for Dublin. This was Mayo, Kildare, Tyrone, Cork – all those days rolled into one and presented as evidence of who they were. Gilroy addressed the question at length in the press conference afterwards.

'If I really believe that [the team is mentally weak] then I should walk out the door here and never be in front of this team,' he said. 'This team has more character and more guts to put up with the kind of stuff that

ABOVE
Bernard Brogan
celebrates his
goal early in the
second half of
the league final.

OPPOSITE
Paul Flynn after
Dublin lost an
eight-point lead
in the league final.

surrounds them every day. And they get back out there and they train and they work. And I'll tell you, they are the most honest guys.

'They will get stick for this. It was an eight-point lead and they lost. People will say what you've just said and we'll deal with that and we have to deal with it because that's our job. We are the Dublin team and we have to listen to that. And when we have the All Ireland, some day, that's when we'll stop hearing that.

'That's the challenge. Because that's what everyone is going to think but I know what's in that dressing room. They have serious character and anyone who questions it, well, they might get a surprise. Some day. But, in fairness, that question is well-asked and it is going to be asked every day for the next two months and it is up to us to answer it during the summer. It is as simple as that.'

And with that, they were off into the summer. A little bit cranky, a little bit cross, but knowing well that this need only be a speedbump and nothing more. If the rest of the country thought they were serial chokers, good luck to them. Gilroy and his squad knew different.

'When we have
the All Ireland,
some day, that's
when we'll stop
hearing that.'

THE CHAPTER THREE CHAMPIONSHIP BEGINS

May is a flat road. Always is these days if you're a Dublin footballer. Last time they kicked a championship ball in May, Longford got a timbering in the first round of Leinster back in 2005. But seeding and general strength mean it needs little short of catastrophe now for them to have to show up on stage before the Leinster quarter-final, so for the players May is a holding pattern. Refuel, restitch, realign. Then go again in June.

Managers live a different life, though. Different calls on their time, different arrows whizzing past their ear. For Pat Gilroy, the month had small hills to climb but they were hills all the same. The panel had to be nipped and tucked back for the summer, so Paddy Andrews, Pat Burke, Blaine Kelly and Alan Hubbard all melted back into society. Few things can better suck the enjoyment out of a championship than having to tell players they won't be enjoying it with you.

For those who remained, there was a squad weekend in London courtesy of Vodafone on the third weekend of the month, four days after the first training session since the league final. They took in a visit to the McLaren Mercedes Formula One team on the Friday before spending the full Saturday training at London Irish's facilities in Surrey. A Sunday morning run-out against local club Parnells shook the previous day from their legs and no more. There's little point making anyone blush by printing the scoreline.

All the while, the questions hovered. Why hadn't they been able to do it when it mattered at the end of the Cork game? If this was a new Dublin – and very few doubted that it was – then why the same old failings? When the championship previews came and went in the papers around the start of the month, it was Cork and Kerry who were the names that topped most of the lists. A Dublin pick would have taken bravado above

45

Few things can better suck the enjoyment out of a championship than having to tell players they won't be enjoying it with you.

and beyond what most people had the stomach or the manners for.

Gilroy wasn't spared a shelling after the league final collapse. His bad luck in losing Bernard Brogan and Bryan Cullen to injury during that second half was no shield either. Far from it. His team had leaked an eight-point lead in the space of half an hour and Cork hadn't even needed to cut corners with a goal or two. The injuries were part of the story but they weren't the part that stuck in your head afterwards. Gilroy knew as much and didn't try to deflect the criticism.

'Losing Bernard was a big factor but we definitely lost any grip we had around the middle third when Bryan went off. We lost all our shape. It was unfair putting in more immature guys. They were in great form but in the context of where that game was at, we should have put in – even if they were defenders – more experienced guys for the game that it was. But it's lessons learned for us all.'

That phrase again. Lessons learned. He hated it and by now the players were no fans either. 'Hopefully one of these days we'll learn something,' said a wry Alan Brogan after the league final. Coming from a man who had already spent close to a decade pushing the boulder up the hill, the implication was obvious. One of these days can turn into none of these days very quickly.

On their return from London, Gilroy anointed Cullen as his captain for the summer. As a message to the world about what he wanted his Dublin to represent, it couldn't have been more straightforward. Be strong. Be skilful. Work till you weep. And above all, keep your head. 'He's just a really calm individual,' said Gilroy. 'More than anyone, it was his loss in the league final that really hurt us.'

A year previously, Cullen wasn't even a starter when their 2010 championship kicked off against Wexford. Go back a few years more and he wasn't a forward either. He fell between all sorts of stools – too classy for most folk to be comfortable with him wearing a low number on his back, too used to anchoring the half-back line to be forced against his will to site himself further forward. In the end, Gilroy settled on having him patrol the area between the 45s – a linkman when they had the ball, a breaker-upper when they hadn't.

'It's funny,' Cullen said. 'People always think I'm being played out of position but I've probably played more of my football at wing-forward than I have at centre-back. When I hang up my boots, I will probably be more remembered as a forward than a back. I did envisage myself playing six until the end of the career. But things change. Different managers come in with different ideas. At the end of the day, it's all about the team and where lads can slot in to make a better team rather than where suits me.'

So. As Gilroy came to the start of June, he had his panel and he had his captain. It was time to inch towards settling on his team. Choices were faced and faced down throughout the line-up. Rory O'Carroll hadn't played a competitive game for Dublin since the All Ireland semi-final defeat to Cork the previous August, but since they intended the road to be a long one this summer, he was going to have to take his first step along it at some point. There was bound to be rust but then rust will only disappear through vigorous scraping. Given that Laois were likely to send Donie Kingston into the fray at some point, it was the least O'Carroll could expect.

The other big call in defence went the way of a championship debutant. James McCarthy had been in and around the panel for two seasons and had won an All Ireland under-21 medal in 2010. Son of 1970s stalwart John McCarthy, the Ballymun Kickhams man came in at wing-back. For neither the first nor last time, Gilroy stressed the qualities he was after in his choice. 'James is a very level-headed young fella,' he said. Where the Dublin manager is concerned, you'd be hard-pushed to locate higher praise.

Despite scoring 1–4 in an A versus B game in Kiltipper the previous week, Mossy Quinn lost his league final place to the returning Alan Brogan. Eoghan O'Gara had also gone on the rampage in that training game, leaving Gilroy in a pretty comfortable chair as he went into the championship. Being able to leave in-form players kicking their heels on the bench wasn't a problem he was especially used to. He was sure he could learn to live with it.

'James is a very level-headed young fella,' he said. Where the Dublin manager is concerned, you'd be hard-pushed to locate higher praise.

OVERLEAF
Newly appointed captain Bryan Cullen leads the team out.

Laois came into the game as an unknown quantity. With Justin McNulty in his first year over the team, nobody was expecting flashing lights and klaxons, and yet they'd taken just about as much out of the league as had been on offer. They had chiselled out promotion from Division Two but let Donegal put too much clear water between them in the first half of a dour league final. Despite reeling them in and playing the best football of the day in the second half, they'd still come out on the wrong side of a 2–11 to 0–16 scoreline.

They hadn't been entirely convincing in the first round of Leinster either. Longford had come to Portlaoise and played into the teeth of a gale in the first half but had held their own. Coming off the back of a successful Division Three campaign, they'd bounced out for the second half sensing blood in the water. With just 20 minutes to go, the sides were level and the home crowd were getting on Laois's back. To pull out a one-point win from there with the deck almost completely stacked against them didn't win McNulty's side any points for style but it would have felt worth a half-dozen five-point strolls.

Truth is, nobody knew exactly what to expect from Laois. They hadn't lost a championship match in Croke Park since 2008 but McNulty had flushed the side with a plethora of new faces since then so it wasn't a particularly relevant statistic. We would just have to suck it and see.

If there was mystery, however, Dublin sought to rub all doubt from

OPPOSITE & ABOVE
Diarmuid Connolly
went on the
rampage in the
first half, forcing
two fine saves from
the Laois keeper
early on before
grabbing a goal
in the 26th minute.

the game right from the off. They burst from the gate like they'd overheard the Laois dressing room say something about their mothers in the team-talk. They were 0–4 to 0–0 up after 10 minutes and Laois were damn lucky to be able to still see them on the horizon. Indeed, it was only the speed and agility of their goalkeeper Eoin Culliton that kept the game alive at all.

Twice in the first five minutes, Culliton pulled off incredible saves from Diarmuid Connolly to prevent a couple of Dublin goals. A month or so earlier, the Schalke goalkeeper Manuel Neuer had put in a night of heroics to deny Manchester United a cricket score in the Champions League semi-final and it seemed for a while that Culliton was going to do the same. By the time Connolly finally beat him in the 26th minute, it was hard not to feel sorry for him. Rarely had a goalkeeper come closer to earning an All Star nomination in one half of football.

'Those were exceptional saves that the Laois 'keeper pulled off,' said Gilroy afterwards, 'because those shots were really hit low and hard into

the corners. But I wasn't that worried about them because we were still creating the chances and, in fairness to Diarmuid, he eventually scored one. I don't think it affected the team. They kept doing what they were doing.'

Though Laois had weathered the initial storm, nobody imagined they could have left the hatches unbattened for the rest of the day and survived. They got back to within a point but after Connolly's goal the result felt inevitable. Even when Laois came out and scored the first three points after half-time to reduce the margin to just two, there was never any real sense that Dublin had a major wobble in them.

As if to underline the point, Dublin put the next seven scores in a row together with the ease of kids lacing daisies in a meadow. Alan Brogan skipped around Croke Park like a player reborn, picking up his first Man of the Match bauble of the summer along the way. And Connolly got into one of those grooves where the posts seemed to bend to accommodate whatever shot he chose to hit at them. Laois didn't raise a flag for 23 minutes and went down to a 1–16 to 0–11 defeat. Their Leinster championship was over and Dublin's had begun.

All of Gilroy's big calls had come off for him, albeit McCarthy had looked a little jittery in possession at times. But O'Carroll had passed with honours even when Kingston had been introduced at half-time, and both Quinn and O'Gara had contributed plenty off the bench. If the team had needed a good day to wash the league final off them, then it did the management no harm to have one either.

'I think the emphasis for us has been to try and get people you will be more sure of how they are going to perform,' said Gilroy afterwards. 'At the end of the day, you can't dictate that. We left guys off the starting 15 this time who were in very good form. Apart from Ross [McConnell], who is only back with us, the other four lads who came on have been playing exceptionally well for us.

'So we were leaving guys off who were in form so you are fairly confident when they came in they were going to do the job. Even in the league final, those fellas were playing pretty well coming into that match, but in the context of the game we probably got it wrong that day. I think you can blame us when it doesn't work.'

'We left guys off the starting 15 this time who were in very good form.'

PREVIOUS SPREAD
Alan Brogan, right,
was man of the match.

Even with a 10-point win under their belts, there were plenty of nits to pick for Dublin. They went through a harum-scarum spell early in the second half when they couldn't win any of Stephen Cluxton's kick-outs. Normally the wellspring for most of what's good about them, they lost four in a row as Laois came back at them.

Culliton's heroics took their toll on Dublin's shooting stats as well. By the end, he'd pulled off four excellent saves and caused the Dublin forwards to think twice about working the ball in so close to him. Dublin finished the day with 17 scores from 35 chances. It was sufficient unto the day that was in it but it hardly needed saying that it wouldn't be sufficient unto every day from that point on.

Still, the first day was for the getting through and Dublin had done that much at least. The flat road was behind them now. From here on, the gradient would only get steeper.

BELOW
Eoghan O'Gara, back
from injury, made a
useful contribution
from the bench.

LEINSTER SFC QUARTER-FINAL
CROKE PARK, 5 JUNE 2011
DUBLIN 1–16, LAOIS 0–11

DUBLIN: Stephen Cluxton (0-3, all 45s); Philly McMahon, Rory O'Carroll, Mick Fitzsimons; James McCarthy, Ger Brennan, Kevin Nolan; Michael Darragh Macauley, Barry Cahill; Paul Flynn, Kevin McManamon, Bryan Cullen (0-1); Alan Brogan (0-2), Diarmuid Connolly (1-3), Bernard Brogan (0-5, 0-1 free). Subs: Paul Casey for Nolan (14-18 mins, blood sub), Denis Bastick for Cahill (43), Eoghan O'Gara for McManamon (47), Tomás Quinn (0-1, free) for B Brogan (63), Ross McConnell for Macauley (66), Declan Lally (0-1) for Cullen (69)

LAOIS: Eoin Culliton; Cahir Healy, Pádraig McMahon (0-2), Mark Timmons; Darren Strong, Shane Julian, Peter O'Leary; Kevin Meaney, Brendan Quigley; Daithí Carroll (0-2), Colm Begley (0-1), Niall Donoher; Ross Munnelly (0-4, 0-2 frees), Billy Sheehan, John O'Loughlin. Subs: Donie Kingston for Sheehan (half-time); Kieran Lillis for O'Loughlin (52 mins); Gary Kavanagh (0-2) for Carroll (54); Conor Boyle for Timmons (61)

Referee: Joe McQuillan (Cavan)

AN UNWANTED EPIC

Summer cracked through the sky for a spell. Not too long, mind, just enough to stop us griping for a weekend or so. The most common line of thinking going into Dublin's Leinster semi-final against Kildare was that the championship needed waking up. It needed an epic.

Pat Gilroy didn't need an epic. A medic perhaps, but not an epic. Although the win over Laois had been humdrum enough, Dublin had still been charged a tariff for coming through it. Corner-back Philly McMahon had ruptured the medial ligament in his right knee in the first half of the game but had been strapped up at the break and played the second half wearing a heavy bandage. It turned out to be dedication above and beyond the call of duty, and a scan a few days after the match told him he'd need at least a month away from the game to fix it.

This was a stick in Dublin's spokes, no question. Ever since the Wexford game at the start of the 2010 Leinster championship, Gilroy had named the same full-back line for every game. Along with Rory O'Carroll and Mick Fitzsimons, McMahon made up the most secure line on the Dublin team. In fact, only once in that period had any of them been so much as substituted, McMahon the one to make way with 15 minutes to go as Meath ran riot and put five goals past them in the previous year's Leinster semi-final.

The upshot was that not only would Gilroy be disrupting one of the foundation stones of the side, he'd have to replace McMahon with somebody with no recent championship experience. A strength and conditioning coach in his day job, McMahon was hardy and he was fast. He wouldn't be easily replaced.

Gilroy got more bad news between the Laois and Kildare matches when it was confirmed that his vice-captain Paul Griffin would be out for the rest of the year with a cruciate tear. Griffin, who had missed the

OPPOSITE
Vice-captain Paul
Griffin reinjured his
knee in a challenge
match; Gilroy, wanting
to keep him around the
squad, asked him to
work with Ray Boyne
compiling stats and
noticing patterns
during matches.

whole of the 2010 championship because of the injury, had made a comeback in a pre-championship challenge match against Monaghan in Parnell Park at the end of May but had developed further complications with it since then.

Griffin had been through everything with Dublin. He caught the tail-end of the Tommy Lyons era and soldiered through every minute of the Pillar Caffrey years as well. He had five Leinster titles to his name but he'd been there for all the beatings too. Now here he was, at the age of 28, about to have a second year in succession wiped from his career. Anyone who spoke to him was struck by how remarkably okay he was with it all. It might have had something to do with him being a qualified physiotherapist. Understanding the nature of the journey must save you asking if we're there yet.

Gilroy was adamant that someone of his temperament and experience shouldn't be lost to the squad for the summer. He asked Griffin to stay around and found him a job helping Ray Boyne compile statistics during the matches. His job would be to sit in one of the corporate boxes in the Upper Hogan and look for patterns to feed into the game plan. It wasn't how he envisaged helping Dublin win an All Ireland but, given that this would be his second summer on crutches, it was plenty.

'Look, it would be nice to be involved in playing football but those things happen,' he told the *Irish Examiner*. 'You get injured. It's just one of those things. It's about dealing with it as a group. You'd like to be there to help guys perform but you just have to find a way to deal with it.'

For Gilroy, Kildare posed different questions from Laois. Tougher questions. Kieran McGeeney was in his third year as their manager and if ever a team played in their overlord's image this Kildare team surely did. They never stopped going, never shirked a tackle, sweated till they were soaked through. When they hit you, you stayed hit.

'You get injured. It's just one of those things. It's about dealing with it as a group. You'd like to be there to help guys perform but you just have to find a way to deal with it.'

They'd come to the Leinster semi-final by way of comfortable victories over Wicklow and Meath, the main spot on their bibs being the inordinate number of wides they'd racked up in both games. Against Wicklow in Portlaoise, they had kicked 17 wides but had at least had the excuse of trying to carry out their business with a gale blowing diagonally across the pitch.

Against Meath, there had been no such defence. They had put Seamus McEnaney's side away on a scoreline of 0–16 to 0–10 but they'd still managed to draw 18 outstretched arms from the umpires (or 36, if you want to get technical about it). McGeeney was happy to shrug the numbers off with a casual insistence that he preferred his players to be shooting than to be dithering but still you fancied that behind closed doors his players were getting plenty of target practice.

All those wides sounded ugly in the abstract, but what they meant in reality was that Kildare were creating far more than their share of scoring chances. Sixteen points and 18 wides against Meath meant an average of a shot at the posts every two minutes.

All of which made Gilroy's choice of Paul Conlon to replace McMahon an eyebrow-raiser. The 28-year-old from Kilmacud Crokes had been on the panel for a couple of seasons and had seen gametime during the 2010 league campaign. But he hadn't featured in that year's championship and nor, despite the amount of injuries and absentees, had he kicked a ball in the 2011 league. Paul Brogan and Nicky Devereux had played a lot during the league but they were overlooked here for what was Conlon's championship debut.

It was big call from Gilroy but he was getting used to making them and wasn't shy about them either. Despite Kevin McManamon being one of the stars of the league campaign, he lost his place for the Kildare game to Eoghan O'Gara. When pushed as to the thinking behind it, Gilroy dropped a weighty hint as to how McManamon was going to be used for the rest of the summer. 'We've had a number of games internally here and Eoghan's been playing very well,' he said. 'It was just impossible to leave him off the team. Kevin is still a very big part of what we're looking to do this year.'

It was big call from Gilroy but he was getting used to making them and wasn't shy about them either.

The suspicion that what he had in mind was to keep McManamon in reserve and only unleash him as a direct-running threat when games had loosened up would take another couple of games to be confirmed. As it turned out, arguably Dublin's best player in the league didn't start another game all year after the Laois one. He would have his say, though.

Kildare threw everything and more at Dublin on the day. It was bruising stuff at times – Michael Darragh Macauley broke his finger so badly in the first half that the bone came out through the skin. Needless to say, he didn't appear after the break, with Eamon Fennell taking his place.

By then, Dublin appeared to be in full control, having gone in at half-time 1–7 to 0–4 up. Gilroy's big selection calls looked to be working well again. Conlon had done such a job on Alan Smith that McGeeney had withdrawn the Kildare corner-forward before half-time. O'Gara hadn't had quite the same level of success but he was at least making a nuisance of himself in a Dublin forward line that had the Kildare backs in a tizzy for most of the first half.

Dublin's goal came from Paul Flynn, who had robbed Gary White and played a one-two with the excellent Alan Brogan before finishing to the net. Their play had been measured throughout that first half, building patiently, while Kildare were far too eager to launch a high ball into their full-forward line. Rory O'Carroll had a field day

OPPOSITE
Diarmuid Connolly after missing a goal chance early on.

BELOW
Michael Darragh Macauley broke his finger in the first half and did not reappear after the break.

OPPOSITE TOP
Paul Flynn
scores a first-half
goal despite being
pushed in the back.

OPPOSITE BOTTOM
Eoghan O'Gara
picked up a second
yellow card for this
foul and was sent
off; Kildare then
clawed their way
back into the game.

back there, collecting and gathering with the ease of a park attendant on a still summer Tuesday.

The whole tenor of the match changed five minutes into the second half, however. O'Gara had picked up a yellow card in the first half for flailing and fouling just a little too tactlessly a little too often. When he launched into another one to stop a Kildare attack – again, his crime was more to do with a lack of subtlety than anything malicious – David Coldrick had to go for the card again. It was silly from the Dublin full-forward, especially after Gilroy had put such faith in him.

Kildare rattled off the first four points in the half to make the scoreline 1–7 to 0–8 and now we had a game on our hands. The teams swapped points again and by the 53rd minute we'd seen seven points scored in the second half without a wide to accompany them. The intensity was high, the quality equally so. For those who were complaining of a sleepy summer, this was water being splashed on their faces.

That didn't suit Dublin at all. Twenty minutes ago, this had been a cakewalk and they set about making it so again. Flynn and Alan Brogan were outstanding, continually breaking up Kildare play around the middle and going for the jugular as soon as they were in possession. When Brogan kicked a fine point on 63 minutes, the stadium more or less breathed out. Crisis averted, everyone back to your corners.

But then out of nowhere, Eamon Callaghan turned the whole farrago on its head. Having started the game at wing-back for Kildare, Callaghan had moved into the forward line during the second half. With two minutes left on the clock, he'd somehow found an avenue of space right down the centre of the Dublin defence, and when no defender came to hunt him off it he scuttled a low skidding shot into the bottom corner of Stephen Cluxton's net.

His crime was more to do with a lack of subtlety than anything malicious – David Coldrick had to go for the card again. It was silly from the Dublin full-forward, especially after Gilroy had put such faith in him.

When he managed to work the space to kick the equalizing point a minute into injury-time, nothing made sense any more. This game was over, then it wasn't. Kildare were dead, then they weren't. With hardly anything left on the clock, we were all fully prepared to go away and try to work out what had happened before coming back for a replay six days later.

But referee Coldrick had other ideas. Dublin launched one last attack and sent one final diagonal ball into Bernard Brogan's corner of the pitch. As he ran out to chase it, there was small but undeniable contact between him and his marker Aindriú Mac Lochlainn. It was a marginal call at best – Brogan didn't even go to ground – and to whistle for it with the sides level took serious *cojones* on Coldrick's part. Or at least that sounded a little like a translation of what the Kildare fans were saying to him as he left the field after Brogan kicked the free and nabbed the win.

'I can't go on about referees much longer,' said a broken McGeeney afterwards. 'I just can't. He [Mac Lochlainn] didn't do anything wrong. Even after probably seven replays, he still didn't do anything wrong.'

Gilroy would have had a certain sympathy with McGeeney's view on the consistency of the refereeing. But on the decision itself, he could find no common ground.

'I think Bernard was probably due a free at that stage,' said Gilroy. 'He probably had a few calls go against him. I think there were seven or eight that he could have had before that. But yer man was pulling him. We either want to have good forwards pulled and have that as part of the game or else it was a free. He was pulling him, there's no question. But Bernard was pulled maybe eight other times as well and he didn't get frees. We either have it as part of the game or we don't.'

In the end, Dublin had been able to open their top button and loosen their tie just enough to get some air in. They came away from Croke Park knowing that the result had been the right one but the road there had been far twistier than it needed to be. June was passing to July and still they yearned for a performance they could hang their hat on.

DUBLIN: Stephen Cluxton (0–2, 0–1 free, 0–1 45); Paul Conlon, Rory O'Carroll, Mick Fitzsimons; James McCarthy, Ger Brennan, Kevin Nolan; Michael Darragh Macauley, Denis Bastick; Paul Flynn (1–1), Alan Brogan (0–2), Bryan Cullen (0–1); Diarmuid Connolly, Eoghan O'Gara, Bernard Brogan (0–6, 0–5 frees). Subs: Eamon Fennell for Macauley (half-time); Kevin McManamon for Connolly (54 mins); Declan Lally for Flynn (62 mins); Ross McConnell for Bastick (66 mins); Barry Cahill for Cullen (68 mins)

KILDARE: Shane Connolly; Michael Foley, Hugh McGrillen, Ollie Lyons; Eamon Callaghan (1–2), Gary White, Emmet Bolton (0–1); Johnny Doyle (0–1, free), Hugh Lynch; Morgan O'Flaherty, Eoin O'Flaherty (0–4, 0–1 free), Pádraig O'Neill; James Kavanagh, Ronan Sweeney (0–1), Alan Smith. Subs: Aindriú Mac Lochlainn for White (29 mins); Rob Kelly (0–2) for Smith (29 mins); Conor Brophy for Lyons (39 mins); Seán Hurley for Sweeney; Tomás O'Connor for Hurley (65 mins)

Referee: Cormac Reilly (Meath)

FLYING UNDER THE RADAR

CHAPTERFIVE

You can't make people care. They have to come around by their own free will. Dublin were in another Leinster final, looking to be crowned champions for the fiftieth time. But the city was almost entirely unmoved. With their Leinster final against Wexford down to take place on the same afternoon as the Munster hurling final, it was hardly surprising that it did not top the bill on the day. The 2 p.m. throw-in only gave the city more reason to showcase its indifference.

County Board chairman Andy Kettle was grumpy about it all. This was unusual for him, for although it often looked to the untrained eye as though he might not be terribly far away from a grumpy state, Andy Kettle was actually having the time of his life. A short stocky man with an impeccably groomed silver moustache that gave him a look not unlike that of British actor Windsor Davies, Kettle had taken over as Dublin county chairman just before Christmas. As a Fingal Ravens man, he'd been involved in the GAA in Dublin for 55 years and had come to the top job a year into his retirement.

He'd already hit the jackpot when the Dublin hurlers had won the National League back in April, and although they'd just taken a thrashing from Kilkenny in the Leinster final, Kettle could still reflect on a summer that was going inordinately well so far. The seniors and minors in both codes had made the Leinster final, and GAA in the city was doing far more to grab people's attention than had been the case for years.

But in the week between the two finals, Kettle pointed out that the Dublin walk-up crowd is used to 4 p.m. starts and warned that the attendance for the football would be well down on other years. 'Unfortunately when the powers-that-be sit down at the start of the

OPPOSITE
Alan Brogan
steams past
Wexford
midfielder
Daithí Waters

OPPOSITE
This fan coveted
Sam Maguire – but
a different trophy
was on offer in the
Leinster final.

OVERLEAF
Croke Park was not
packed for the Leinster
final – a marker of the
state of the economy
and of the fans'
wariness.

year to work out television schedules that is where the problem starts,' Kettle told *The Irish Times*.

Now, this was true and it wasn't true. The last time the Leinster final saw a full house – the last three times, in fact – the throw-in had indeed been around the four o'clock mark. But just because a grey dog barks doesn't mean only a grey dog will bark. The reason you couldn't get a seat for a Leinster final between 2006 and 2008 wasn't because of a big walk-up crowd, it was because going to see Dublin at the height of summer was something the people of city could afford to do in huge numbers back then. In 2006, Dublin v Offaly was completely sold out on the Thursday before the game, and that would have been the case regardless of the time of the throw-in. That was the world we lived in back then.

Things were different now, three years into a brutal recession. Though the GAA had done their best to keep ticket prices reasonable through the summer, it was still a reach to hope for anything like the same number of people through the gates. The Leinster Council were aiming for anything over 50,000. In the event, the figure was 43,983.

That number was down by over 30,000 on the last time Dublin were in a Leinster final, in 2009 – a game which also threw-in at 2 p.m., by the by. Just as worryingly, it was down by around 5,000 on the 2010 final between Meath and Louth. This was about more than walk-up crowds and TV coverage and even the recession. A reality had to be faced. Between one thing and another, the Dubs just weren't the draw they used to be.

Not enough people believed, not yet anyway. They'd been burned for believing before and it would take a while for them to find it within them again. Losing the league final to the All Ireland champions was no big deal but losing it from eight points up with half an hour left most assuredly was. It was just such a Dublin way to lose a game – careless, panicky, dumb even at times. It belonged to a time Pat Gilroy was trying to leave behind.

> Not enough people believed, not yet anyway. They'd been burned for believing before and it would take a while for them to find it within them again.

And then they'd been blessed to survive a Kildare game that they'd done their best to throw away as well. Again, the problem was more storyline than scoreline. Kildare were a top-five side, so eking out a one-point win over them was nothing to get down in the mouth about. But Dublin had coughed up a four-point lead with two minutes to go and had been spared a replay only by an uncommonly benign referee. They'd been the better team, but still it felt as though the result carried an asterisk.

The cold truth was that winning a Leinster title wouldn't change anyone's mind. They'd won Leinster titles before and it had got them nowhere. Nowhere new at any rate. The feeling among Dublin supporters was that while people could talk Wexford up as much

as they liked, this was still a final Gilroy's side ought to win. But if it led to being beaten by the first good team they met, then what was the point in getting excited?

As it happened, Wexford didn't need to be talked up. Fair enough, they'd come through the easier side of the draw but you couldn't have imagined any team doing so in better style. They'd put up a remarkable 7–52 in three matches against Offaly, Westmeath and Carlow. Just as impressive was the fact that they hadn't conceded a goal yet. Jason Ryan had put together a fast and nimble young team who knew they were coming to Dublin with nobody outside of their own county giving them a chance.

Ryan was a prodigy among county managers. When Pat Gilroy was winning an All Ireland on the pitch for Dublin in 1995, Ryan was still in school. He'd managed Wexford to an All Ireland semi-final in 2008 when he was just 32, and his players had an obvious bond with him. For them to be running up such huge scores a couple of years after the retirement of former Footballer of the Year Mattie Forde was no accident. They were prepared for everything, with players given files before games on their opposite numbers. Ryan was coming to Croke Park to take a trophy home.

He wasn't above throwing the odd pebble in the pond to see how it would ripple out. There had been a few days of wailing about referees in the aftermath of the free David Coldrick had given at the end of the Kildare game, so Ryan made sure in the week before the final to remind Joe McQuillan that people would be watching him referee two teams and not just one.

'There is no point in beating about the bush, but Bernard Brogan got a few soft frees in that game,' he said. 'We are just hoping that if Bernard Brogan gets soft frees in the final that Ben Brosnan, Ciarán Lyng, Shane Roche and Red Barry will get soft frees too. All we are asking for is consistency from the referee – that it is not one rule for Dublin and another rule for Wexford. His decision-making has to be across the board.'

When Pat Gilroy was winning an All Ireland on the pitch for Dublin in 1995, Ryan was still in school.

PREVIOUS SPREAD
Eoghan O'Gara,
shooting high, got
the nod from Gilroy
despite coming off
his second red card
of the year.

OPPOSITE TOP
Rory O'Carroll
punches the ball
away from Wexford
corner-forward
Redmond Barry.

OPPOSITE BOTTOM
Redmond Barry's
goal capped a burst
in which Wexford
went from four
points behind to
three points ahead.

For Gilroy, it was already an old argument and not one he wanted to waste time getting into, for he had more pressing concerns. Michael Darragh Macauley's broken finger was going to keep him out of the final, so for the third straight game Gilroy was unable to name an unchanged side. In came Eamon Fennell to partner Denis Bastick, with the manager pronouncing Fennell 'the best high fielder of a ball we have in the squad'.

Fennell's story was an interesting one. Outside the county he was more famous for what he wasn't than what he was. He'd been through a two-year battle to get a transfer from O'Tooles to St Vincent's and had missed out on playing for Dublin in the early part of Gilroy's reign as a result. The case had finally been sorted out in February and he was only now making a proper breakthrough for Dublin. He was loud and brash and popular in the squad, a part-time DJ when he wasn't playing football.

Gilroy handed him the start, and did the same with Eoghan O'Gara despite the sending off that had changed the game against Kildare. Because he been dismissed with two yellow cards rather than a straight red, O'Gara hadn't picked up a ban and was free to play in the final, but Gilroy had to tackle questions as to the wisdom of sticking with him. 'We've been doing work with him for the last two weeks,' he conceded. 'A big part of it is down to how strong he is. If he puts his arm on somebody, they fall over. Another fella does it, it's nothing. He just has to be conscious of it.'

The game itself was one of those that left nobody happy. Dublin were sluggish and one-paced throughout. Wexford gave them their fill of it and still came away beaten. They actually led with 25 minutes to go after a Redmond Barry goal topped off a 20-minute spell either side of half-time where they outscored Dublin by 1–4 to 0–0. Substitute Kevin McManamon dragged Dublin back into the game, stopping the rot with a good point in the 46th minute, just after the Wexford goal.

The game itself was one of those that left nobody happy. Dublin were sluggish and one-paced throughout. Wexford gave them their fill of it and still came away beaten.

Points by Bryan Cullen and Bernard Brogan followed, but it took a freak goal to put them on top. When Wexford goalkeeper Anthony Masterson came to punch a high ball in on top of the full-back line, he succeeded only in batting it off his full-back Graeme Molloy and the deflection took it into the Wexford goal. At a stroke, Wexford's advantage was wiped out: Dublin now led 1–9 to 1–8. Alan Brogan – who was having another outstanding game – scored the next point soon after, and then wing-back James McCarthy finished the job with a fine goal after he ran untouched into the Wexford square. The second goal was what ultimately separated the teams.

At the end, the Dublin players barely raised an arm in triumph. It was another provincial title but it was comfortably their worst display of the summer. Not only had all three players in their full-forward line been substituted, one of their replacements – Mossy Quinn – had later been taken off himself.

PREVIOUS SPREAD
Bryan Cullen, Delaney
Cup in hand, greets
fans afterwards; next
up, the quest for a
more important
piece of silverware.

Most worryingly of all from a Dublin point of view, Bernard Brogan was close to hapless at times. Apart from his opening score – a barely believable shot from under the Cusack Stand – he shot wide and he shot short and generally had a three-out-of-10 afternoon before being called ashore with 10 minutes to go. Baffling.

'We didn't perform well,' said Gilroy in the press conference afterwards. 'We had a situation where Bernard Brogan was winning the ball and getting shots off but he'd 11 chances that he didn't score. That's a very unusual situation but he wasn't doing anything for the team and it wasn't going to change. Only for Eoghan O'Gara getting an injury we might have taken Bernard off a bit earlier. He is human. He's allowed to have the odd off-day, and in fairness to him he hasn't done that for a long, long time.

'And yet the team just kept plugging away. Guys came in. I think Barry Cahill did very well when he did and Kevin McManamon was one of the game-changers. He started to get the ball and beat men, which I think was crucial for us. Wexford put us under tremendous pressure all the time when we were shooting today. And our shooting was very poor. I don't think we've created as many chances in a game and missed as many all year. We got the ball into their scoring area 45 times, and 33 times we got nothing off it. So we needed to change it. It was one of those days when things weren't running for those fellas.'

All in all, a grim mood hung over the Dublin team after the game. Stephen Cluxton didn't even wait to see the cup lifted, he just walked straight down the tunnel after the game. A day and a performance to forget.

'Certainly, there will be no one tipping us to win the All Ireland after that performance,' said Bryan Cullen. 'No harm to come in under the radar a little bit. That's going to refocus lads hugely. We have a lot of work to do. You can see that in both halves. Maybe we're not as good as we think we are.'

If that was indeed the case, then Dublin's summer wasn't going to last for very much longer.

'Certainly, there will be no one tipping us to win the All Ireland after that performance.'

LEINSTER SFC FINAL
CROKE PARK, 10 JULY 2011
DUBLIN 2–12, WEXFORD 1–12

DUBLIN: Stephen Cluxton (0–1, 45); Paul Conlon, Rory O'Carroll, Mick Fitzsimons; James McCarthy (1–0), Ger Brennan, Kevin Nolan; Denis Bastick (0–1), Eamon Fennell; Paul Flynn (0–1), Alan Brogan (0–3), Bryan Cullen (0–1); Diarmuid Connolly, Bernard Brogan (0–3, 0–1 free), Eoghan O'Gara. Subs: Mossy Quinn for Connolly (31 mins); Kevin McManamon (0–1) for O'Gara (half-time); Barry Cahill for Fennell (52 mins); David Henry for Bernard Brogan (61 mins); Ross McConnell (0–1) for Quinn (69 mins)

WEXFORD: Anthony Masterson; Joey Wadding, Graeme Molloy (1–0, own goal), Brian Malone; Adrian Flynn (0–1), David Murphy, Andreas Doyle; Daithí Waters, Rory Quinlivan; Eric Bradley, Ben Brosnan (0–9, 0–5 frees, 0–2 45s), Colm Morris; Ciarán Lyng (0–2), Redmond Barry (1–0), Shane Roche. Subs: PJ Banville for Roche (41 mins); Adrian Morrissey for Doyle (54 mins); Paddy Byrne for Morris (63 mins); Liam Óg McGovern for Quinlivan (64 mins)

ALL CHANGED, CHANGED UTTERLY

CHAPTER SIX

Eight teams left. Kerry v Limerick, Mayo v Cork, Donegal v Kildare, Dublin v Tyrone. Nobody doubted which was the tie of the round, but look for anyone to call it and you'd be looking a long time. Dublin or Tyrone? New breed or old broom?

A month before, there would barely even have been a question. On the weekend that Dublin were getting ready to play the Leinster final, Tyrone were schlepping down the country to play Longford in round two of the qualifiers. Donegal had scuttled them out of Ulster with a late goal from Colm McFadden and the obituarists were getting ready to go through their notes. That Pearse Park was not an easy place to be going in search of a spark for your season had passed into the realm of cliché by now, and Longford were the obvious choice for the upset of the round.

Tyrone escaped with their lives but only after going in a point behind at the break. The Tyrone team that won three All Irelands in six years just never used to do that kind of thing. It was offensive to them to give a sucker an even break, and although Longford were eventually put away, few came out of Pearse Park that night imagining that Mickey Harte's side were going to be long for this championship.

If there was a chink of light, it was down among the agate type at the end of the reports. Of the 1–17 Tyrone accumulated, 1–10 had come from boots belonging to players who didn't have All Ireland senior medals to their name. Peter Harte had scored seven points, all but one from play. Mark Donnelly had chipped in with 1–2, Kyle Coney with a point. Tyrone had waited an age for new blood to come along and challenge the men who'd won those All Irelands. The possibility at least existed now that they might be here.

Still, the fact remained that while Tyrone were wearily heading back north that night to arrive home well past midnight, the serious All Ireland contenders were readying themselves for bigger battles. Kerry and Cork had played out a Munster final of two contrasting halves the previous Sunday, Kerry blitzing the All Ireland champions in the opening half-hour and Cork storming back to almost grab a win by the end. Kildare had torched Laois in a qualifier of their own, and Dublin were about to play in the Leinster final. Did folk really think Tyrone had the measure of any of those four? If they did, they were keeping it to themselves.

But time ticks on and the world turns slowly. Dublin had a whole month to stew in the juices of their Leinster final display. If it was an article of faith that they wouldn't be as bad again, it was nonetheless a worrying time of the year to be on the parabola's downswing rather than the ascent. Bernard Brogan was given a free pass for his off-day against Wexford but something nagged about it all the same. If the Footballer of Year could put in such a poor display, didn't it follow that anyone could? That three or four of them could at the same time?

All the while, the qualifiers were rumbling along at their own speed. On the night of the Leinster final, the draws for rounds three and four were made, with Tyrone pulled out of the drum alongside Armagh, and the winners of that match to go through to meet whoever lost the Connacht final. Nothing stirred the blood of a Tyrone side quite like the thought of facing Armagh in a thump-and-thunder championship game. And after that they would fancy themselves against whoever came out of what looked like a fairly mediocre Connacht championship. From the ashes of what seemed like a lost season, they could see a route to August at least now.

That's the trouble with having a month between the Leinster final and the All Ireland quarter-final. While Dublin twiddled thumbs, Tyrone were able to rebuild their team and their confidence. They put Armagh to the sword in Omagh, beating them 2–13 to 0–13. Then they sent Roscommon home from Croke Park, overcoming a shaky first half to run out 3–19 to 1–14 winners in the end. Two games away from another final, their tails were wagging.

Dublin had a whole month to stew in the juices of their Leinster final display.

All of which meant that the bookies had this one down as close to an even proposition. Dublin were 5–6, Tyrone 6–5. Truth be told, this would have been insulting to Dublin if they hadn't adopted a sticks-and-stones mindset a long time back. Dublin had lost one game all year – in the league, by a point, to the reigning All Ireland champions. Tyrone hadn't been able to get out of Division Two. Dublin had very obviously improved since beating Tyrone 12 months beforehand, whereas Tyrone were a work in progress. Dublin had established youth and pep throughout their side; Tyrone were rushing them into the side like a kid trying to cram for an exam. By any empirical measure, Dublin ought to have been stronger favourites.

But then again, what are bookies' odds if they aren't statements of impression and preconception? Dublin weren't stronger favourites because on the whole they weren't really trusted yet. That they were favourites at all was a sign that they'd made progress since the previous August, but in a winner-takes-all encounter against winners who'd taken it all before, who was willing to close their eyes and take that leap? Plainly, not enough for the weight of money to make them any shorter than 5–6.

Impression and preconception cut both ways, of course. Just as the view of Dublin may have been skewed by what had gone on in the past,

PREVIOUS SPREAD
Bernard Brogan fights
past Tyrone full-back
Joe McMahon.

OPPOSITE
Pat Gilroy and
the officials share
a laugh – but don't
see eye to eye.

so the fancy for Tyrone reflected the fact that they had been here before. If few were exactly ready to anoint them as All Ireland favourites just yet, you knew that all it would take was a win over the Dubs and they'd shoot right to the top of the charts. That's the difference – when you've won the big prize, people cut you some slack. When you haven't won it for 16 years, it takes very little for the rope to tighten.

All Dublin could do was keep on keeping on and remind themselves that regardless of what had happened in the Leinster final, they were still on course. Bryan Cullen had said after the Wexford game that the season started all over again from there on out. However bad the performance, it was history. Watch the DVD, gulp at the stats and move on.

Indeed, it suited Pat Gilroy to be coming into the All Ireland series with people seeing his side as an afterthought. Right from the beginning of his tenure, one thing he'd tried to do was rid the Dublin football team of hype. Too often down the years he'd seen Dublin teams get over-played and over-promoted. He'd seen players who just weren't as good as they thought they were find their actual level at the worst possible moment – on big days in front of huge crowds. It was never pretty, and he figured that if he was able to lower the expectation levels and take the air out of the occasional bouts of drama that surrounded the team, he might be on to something.

So over his three years in charge, he'd done what he could to calm everything down. To deal with the media, he organized weekly 8 a.m. press conferences where he announced his team for the weekend and offered up a player for interviews. The Dublin football team were always going to attract column inches, but this was a way of exerting some measure of control over what was written and broadcast. It meant that neither he nor his players were being plagued for interviews the week of games, that they didn't have to waste energy avoiding numbers they didn't recognize flashing on their phones.

The days of marching en masse down to Hill 16 before games were over, as were the days of gloating at opponents after big scores had gone in.

ABOVE
Kevin Nolan
confronts
Philip Jordan.

OPPOSITE
Denis Bastick
leaves Conor
Gormley in
his wake.

With his squad, he made it clear that the flashy, bombastic days of old were gone. The days of marching en masse down to Hill 16 before games were over, as were the days of gloating at opponents after big scores had gone in. If you scored a goal, your job was to cover your man to stop a quick kick-out. It wasn't to get in the face of the corner-back. There was no need for swagger. Just work, that's all. Just work.

It extended to all aspects of their existence as Dublin footballers. Those 6.30 a.m. training sessions in January weren't just a way to get the players out of bed and teach them the worth of suffering. They were also a way of getting two training sessions a day into them, one in the morning and one in the evening. Come summer, Dublin wouldn't want for fitness and they wouldn't want for work ethic either.

And in the end, work ethic and fitness and the absence of hype all fed into what they did on the pitch. Gilroy's style of play demanded all of this and more. You had to work till you wept, you had to track back as far as was necessary no matter what number was on your shirt. Ten minutes from the end of the Down game in the league, every player on the Dublin team was back in Dublin's half of the pitch. It was hard to crank up a hype machine around a team of diligent worker bees.

'We certainly had to change the way we played a little bit and there was a lot more defensive duties put on the forwards,' Alan Brogan said

in an interview in *The Irish Times*. 'But looking at it now it definitely worked. It took a while to buy into it, alright, like any change takes time to buy into. In fairness to Pat, he asked me to do something, he was not telling me. Like he showed us why we need to do it and what would happen if we did do it and that always makes it easier when you can see the results. Now, as we go on, we can see the results.'

One result was that Brogan himself was well on his way towards emulating the achievement of his kid brother the year before. He was having an outstanding year, man of the match in each of their Leinster championship games. Already it looked nailed on that if Dublin ended the year where they hoped to, the Footballer of the Year award would be staying in the family.

But first they had to deal with Tyrone. And boy, did they deal with them. Dublin 0–22, Tyrone 0–15 – and Tyrone were flattered by the margin. Dublin ate them whole and without salt. They kicked 11 points in each half, 19 of them from play in a performance that was first and foremost about Dubin's utter dominance around the middle of the pitch. With 20 minutes to go, both of Tyrone's starting midfielders and their whole half-forward line had been replaced. Manager Mickey Harte ruefully admitted afterwards that if he'd been allowed to make 10 substitutions he would have.

'Diarmuid is capable
of doing anything.'

PREVIOUS SPREAD
**All smiles for man of
the match Diarmuid
Connolly and his
teammates.**

Yet even as the Dublin midfield dominated and both Brogan brothers fizzed around a wet Croke Park, the evening belonged to Diarmuid Connolly. Seven points, all from play and all kicked with training-ground ease. Tyrone tried three different men on him and they were all embarrassed. Dublin were better than Tyrone in every department but only Connolly was untouchable.

'I think he had a reasonable game alright,' teased Pat Gilroy afterwards. Gilroy is a clubmate of Connolly's at St Vincent's and won an All Ireland club title alongside him in 2008. One of his first acts as Dublin manager had been to send Connolly home from a training week in La Manga in January 2009 for indiscipline. As a statement of intent, it rang out even then. As did the fact that Connolly worked his way back into the good books in time.

'Diarmuid is capable of doing anything,' said Gilroy. 'He is a phenomenal talent. He is capable of doing even better than that. He is that good and we see it out at training. We have been waiting a while for that to come in a big game in Croke Park. He has done well in this year's league, he has committed himself hugely in terms of effort. Outside of the points he scored, his work-rate was phenomenal, I think he stripped the ball three times from Tyrone guys and that is a huge plus as well.'

The result was huge, the performance a warning shot to the championship. Whatever way you spun it, Dublin were now legitimate. They'd sent Tyrone packing for a second year in a row, burnt them at the stake and never looked back. Whatever happened from now on, they would be viewed differently.

All of a sudden, they were two wins away from Valhalla.

Tyrone were flattered by the margin. Dublin ate them whole and without salt.

DUBLIN: Stephen Cluxton (0–2, 0–1 45, 0–1 free); Mick Fitzsimons, Rory O'Carroll, Cian O'Sullivan; James McCarthy, Ger Brennan, Kevin Nolan; Denis Bastick, Michael Darragh Macauley; Paul Flynn (0–2), Barry Cahill (0–1), Bryan Cullen (0–1); Alan Brogan (0–3), Diarmuid Connolly (0–7), Bernard Brogan (0–5, 0–1 free). Subs: Ross McConnell for Macauley (59 mins); Kevin McManamon for Flynn (66 mins); Eamon Fennell for Bastick (69 mins); Philly McMahon for Nolan (71 mins)

TYRONE: Pascal McConnell; Joe McMahon, Justin McMahon, Martin Swift; Seán O'Neill, Conor Gormley, Philip Jordan; Kevin Hughes, Seán Cavanagh (0–4, 0–3 frees); Colm Cavanagh, Brian McGuigan, Peter Harte (0–1, free); Martin Penrose (0–4, 0–3 frees), Mark Donnelly (0–2), Owen Mulligan. Subs: Brian Dooher (0–1) for McGuigan (half-time); Dermot Carlin for Justin McMahon (half-time); Stephen O'Neill (0–2) for Harte (44 mins); Enda McGinley (0–1) for Hughes (52 mins); Aidan Cassidy for Cavanagh (54 mins)

Referee: Joe McQuillan (Cavan)

EVERYBODY WORKS, EVERYBODY FIGHTS

CHAPTER SEVEN

The aftermath of the Tyrone dismantling frothed and bubbled away for days. You couldn't get into a taxi without the driver going, 'WharrraboudaDubs, wha?' Radio shows from *Morning Ireland* to *Off the Ball* gloried the very backness of the Jacks. The *Evening Herald* caught the prevailing tone.

'Dublin's footballers have given the whole city a much-needed lift,' they wrote. 'Saturday's stirring victory against Tyrone has put a smile on people's faces. The trouncing – against the Dubs' bogey team – also highlighted the quality in their ranks. Pat Gilroy's men produced a wonderful display, showing commitment and skill in equal measure.'

That's the problem with lighting up the sky – it's hard to do it unnoticed. The hype that Pat Gilroy had been trying to avoid all along could not be stifled now. The quarter-finals had exploded the championship – Kildare were gone, Cork were gone, Tyrone were gone, leaving Dublin and Kerry on opposite sides of the draw and seemingly fated to meet in the final for the first time since 1985. That was about the last thing Gilroy needed – the country salivating over a final before either semi-final had even been played.

By midweek, the wise men of the written media were counselling caution. 'Perfect time for Gilroy to accentuate the negatives', said the headline above Martin Breheny's piece in the *Irish Independent*. 'The last thing he – and Dublin – need right now is the commentating classes competing with each other in search of the most glowing commendations.' Meanwhile, over in *The Irish Times*, the headline read 'Improving Dublin must still tread with caution'. 'There is terror within the county,' wrote Seán Moran, 'at the very prospect of an accelerating bandwagon ("Dubs won't be deterred by hype – see 12-page special") and especially when Kerry are still around.'

If there was a legacy from the 16 years without an All Ireland, this was maybe the most powerful aspect of it. Having been down this road before, the city and county remembered every twist and turn, every pike and pothole. And unless and until they got to see a Dublin captain in the Hogan Stand with the cup in his hands, they wanted no part of the hysteria. The desire not to tempt fate had become an ache, even among a younger generation who barely remembered 1995 but could give you chapter and verse on 2002, 2006, 2007, 2008 and so on and on and ever on. On Twitter, wisecracks about the Dubs' inexorable progress through the championship came attached to the hashtag #unstoppablejuggernaut. In an ironic way, of course.

On Twitter, wisecracks about the Dubs' inexorable progress through the championship came attached to the hashtag #unstoppablejuggernaut.

OPPOSITE
Pat Gilroy came into
the game expecting
exactly what Dublin
got from Donegal: a
stiflingly defensive
approach.

NEXT SPREAD
Ger Brennan looks
to find a teammate
in space.

On the face of it, coming up against Donegal in the semi-final wasn't going to help matters. Jim McGuinness was bringing a young team to Dublin that had already overachieved for the year. They'd won Division Two of the National League and followed it up with their first Ulster title since 1992. A callow side with a first-year manager, they were surely in bonus territory now.

They didn't run up big scores like Dublin had been doing – their average points-per-game total was 14.8, while Dublin's was 18.5. In fact, if you took out the five points they scored in extra-time against Kildare in their quarter-final, their 70-minute average dipped below 14. If ever there was team on paper that the Dublin public could be forgiven for overlooking, this was it.

Good thing the game isn't played on paper, then. Anyone who had watched Donegal play during the summer knew that this was just about the best possible team to burst the Dublin balloon. McGuinness had put together the most cussed and awkward side the championship had seen for years. No, they hadn't been running up big scores but they'd still won every game in Ulster by at least three points. In the previous 25 years of the Ulster championship, only Tyrone in 1996 and again in 2008 could match such a feat.

The key to Donegal was their defence. Or, more to the point, their defensive system. Every team these days got men back, but nobody got as many back as Donegal. They flooded their defence with at least eight bodies at all times, regularly having up to 11 or 12 behind their own 45-metre line. They marked space instead of marking men. The most any team had scored against them over 70 minutes was Cavan's 1–8.

On top of getting back and crowding out space, Donegal were unbelievably disciplined. They hit hard without giving away scoreable frees – in the five games they'd played before the semi-final (plus the extra-time) they'd conceded only 17 points to free kicks. Long story short: if you were going to score a point against Donegal, you were going to earn it.

Anyone who had watched Donegal play during the summer knew that this was just about the best possible team to burst the Dublin balloon.

Their death-or-glory devotion to defence coupled with the by-now customary nervousness in Dublin at the prospect of making an All Ireland final meant that Gilroy managed to oversee a relatively hype-free build-up to the game. There were a few more flags hanging from windows and attached to cars, but that was about the height of it. The players retreated into their shell and got on with readying themselves for a day in the trenches. So much so that on the Friday before the game, Gilroy could reflect on a job well done and a fire well fought.

'Guys themselves have been looking for a bit of space from people around them,' he said. 'People have respected that and said, "If that's going to help the team perform better then let's give them that bit of space." People maybe have suffocated players in the past and it didn't really work out well for the team. By just giving us a bit of space, certainly the mood is calm and relaxed. Hype certainly hasn't affected us this week. It just hasn't manifested itself. Maybe it's overstated, but in the past players have been suffocated by too much attention close to the game and just weren't able to focus on the game.'

'Hype certainly hasn't affected us this week. It just hasn't manifested itself.'

OPPOSITE
Kevin Nolan and
Denis Bastick contest
a high ball with
Donegal full-forward
Michael Murphy.

For the first time all year, Gilroy was able to name an unchanged side. Michael Darragh Macauley's finger had come through the Tyrone game without a hitch so he continued in midfield. Cian O'Sullivan had been a foot-perfect addition to the full-back line against Tyrone, and although Philly McMahon was fit and recovered by now, Gilroy stuck with what he had. With O'Sullivan and Rory O'Carroll from Kilmacud Crokes and Mick Fitzsimons from Cuala, Dublin now had what Kevin McManamon would come to refer to as 'the poshest full-back line in the world'. All three stood at 6'1" and all three were 23 or younger. It was far from posh they played.

Which was just as well, because it became clear from early on that posh wasn't going to cut it against Donegal. This was a game like nothing anyone had ever seen before. You knew something out of the ordinary was happening when Donegal's number 4, Frank McGlynn, went and stood beside O'Carroll for the throw-in, and no sooner had Maurice Deegan tossed the ball in the air than McGlynn was sprinting the length of the pitch to get back goalside of the action.

With Donegal getting so many men behind the ball, they put the onus on Dublin to find a way through. But since Dublin's default setting had a fair portion of their team back around the half-back line as well, what we were left with was stalemate. Most of the play got choked off between the two 45s with pockets of players crowding the ball like kids in a schoolyard game. After 24 minutes, the score was 0–1 apiece and both points had come from frees.

It was putrid stuff, hard work to watch, never mind play. The Dublin crowd booed Donegal every time they flicked off another handpass – the first time anyone could remember a team being booed at Croke Park on the basis of a tactical innovation rather than a dirty belt – but in truth, there was the pair of them in it. Darragh Ó Sé would say in his

With O'Sullivan and Rory O'Carroll from Kilmacud Crokes and Mick Fitzsimons from Cuala, Dublin now had what Kevin McManamon would come to refer to as 'the poshest full-back line in the world'.

Irish Times column the following week that 'Colm McFadden must have been thinking he was the best footballer in the country because there were times that Dublin had three players marking him.'

By the end of the half, it was clear that Donegal were more comfortable than Dublin in the business of chiselling out scores in a game like this. Ryan Bradley scored the first point from play in the 25th minute and Donegal followed up with one each from McFadden and Kevin Cassidy before the break. Dublin were in a spin, unable to settle into any sort of rhythm. Bernard Brogan kicked a second free but that was all they could manage. Donegal went into half-time 0–4 to 0–2 ahead.

By the end of the half, it was clear that Donegal were more comfortable than Dublin in the business of chiselling out scores in a game like this.

ABOVE
The Donegal
defence gave
Bernard Brogan and
his fellow forwards
no space to work in.

OPPOSITE
Alan Brogan and
Frank McGlynn race
for a loose ball.

Dublin were in trouble, more trouble than they'd been in at any stage since the beginning of the championship. They hadn't spent very much time all year fighting to claw back a deficit. They'd led from start to finish against Laois, Kildare had only managed to inch ahead of them for five minutes in the first half, and they'd swapped leads with Tyrone in the opening skirmishes of the All Ireland quarter-final before pulling away and leaving them for dust. Only against Wexford had they been down by any more than a point at any stage and even then, it took them just seven minutes to close the gap.

All in all, they had spent a sum total of 14 minutes chasing a lead all summer. Now they would have to chase one against the toughest defence in the country. It might only have been two points at the break,

They had spent a sum total of 14 minutes chasing a lead all summer. Now they would have to chase one against the toughest defence in the country.

OPPOSITE
**Bernard Brogan
roars at Hill 16 after
winning a free.**

but on a day like this – without a single score yet from play – two points was an ocean. Not that Gilroy saw any need for alarm at half-time.

'That was one of the easiest team talks I've ever had to give because we were exactly where we thought we would be,' he said afterwards. 'We expected that game. The hard team talks are when you're dealing with something that you don't expect but we knew from the start the kind of test they were going to pose. And all we wanted to do was keep our composure and tweak a few little things. But at no stage in that game did I think we weren't going to find a way. I was very confident it would happen for us.'

Just how confident he would have remained had McFadden's shot a minute after the break gone under the crossbar instead of over is lost to the ages. The Donegal forward probably took his shot a step quicker than he needed to, and though the point put Donegal three ahead – the most Dublin had been led by all year – everyone in the ground knew that the Dubs had just dodged a bullet. A goal in this game was worth far more than three points.

As it was, Dublin stayed set about clawing them back. Stephen Cluxton kicked a free and a 45 that were pure oxygen as the Dubs struggled for breath. McManamon had come on at half-time and was running at defenders instead of trying to play around them. Bernard Brogan kicked a free of his own before a flicking a gorgeous through ball for McManamon to run on to, and the substitute knocked over Dublin's first point from play, a full hour into the game. This came just moments after Diarmuid Connolly had got himself sent off for raising his fist to a Donegal player.

Dublin had been behind for 31 minutes, more than double the length of time they'd trailed in all their other games combined. They had faced a demon and found a way to match it. If they could come through it now

'That was one of the easiest team talks I've ever had to give because we were exactly where we thought we would be.'

and finish out the game, with fourteen men on the pitch, it would feel like a better win than even the Tyrone game. It's one thing finding a victory when everything you touch sails over the bar. Digging one out of a war-zone like this would be another matter altogether.

They were helped by the fact that Donegal didn't have a second card to play. Once Dublin drew level, McGuinness's players got panicky and suddenly looked exhausted. Their system had been set up to eke out a lead and to protect it. When the squeeze came on from Dublin and Bryan Cullen put them ahead with eight minutes to go, Donegal were powerless to react. In the end, Dublin crawled through by 0–8 to 0–6, outscoring Donegal three points to nil after going a man down.

It's one thing finding a victory when everything you touch sails over the bar. Digging one out of a war-zone like this would be another matter altogether.

It had been a grim but fascinating spectacle all the way through. The tension in Croke Park had been palpable. The Donegal players slumped to the turf afterwards, emptied from the effort. And although the dudgeon would be high in the RTÉ studio and the papers would not be kind over the next while, it was hard not feel as though there was something heroic about what they'd done out there.

'I totally admire them,' Gilroy said. 'Totally admire them. Why would you go out and leave a load of space against fellas who kicked 22 points the last day? It was just sensible what they did. You would have to admire them because it's incredible to get a whole group of players into the sort of shape you need to be in to do what they did for so long today.'

For his part, McGuinness was wholly unapologetic. 'Everybody's got an opinion,' he shrugged. 'It's irrelevant to us. For 19 years, Donegal teams would have come here and played a certain brand of football that hasn't served us well. It hasn't brought rewards to fellas who've put in an awful lot of work over those 19 years. We feel now that our lads have a National League medal and an Ulster Championship medal and at 0–6 to 0–3 up we were at a point where we could have pushed on and made it to an All Ireland final. We need to go away now and see can we come back stronger and can we sort out the offensive side of things.

'The pundits have their opinion, the man in the street has his opinion. My job is to put medals in these players' pockets. We've managed to do that twice this year and nearly made an All Ireland final. We'll obviously try to improve ourselves over the winter but we won't be going to Ballybofey and Castlefin for training next year with the intention of making Pat Spillane feel good. That won't be our primary objective.'

You got the feeling Pat Gilroy would have plenty of common ground with McGuinness if they sat down for a chinwag. When he took over Dublin, he instituted something of the attitude McGuinness was instilling in his team: everybody works, everybody fights, everybody gets back to help out. Once you have that, you can evolve.

And now, three years later, it had evolved far enough to bring Dublin to an All Ireland final for the first time in 16 years.

'I totally admire them,' Gilroy said. 'Why would you go out and leave a load of space against fellas who kicked 22 points the last day?'

ALL IRELAND SFC SEMI-FINAL
CROKE PARK, 28 AUGUST 2011
DUBLIN 0-8, DONEGAL 0-6

DUBLIN: Stephen Cluxton (0-2, 0-1 free, 0-1 45); Cian O'Sullivan, Rory O'Carroll, Mick Fitzsimons; James McCarthy, Ger Brennan, Kevin Nolan; Michael Darragh Macauley, Denis Bastick; Paul Flynn, Barry Cahill, Bryan Cullen (0-1); Alan Brogan, Diarmuid Connolly, Bernard Brogan (0-4, all frees). Subs: Philly McMahon for O'Carroll (26 mins); Kevin McManamon (0-1) for Cahill (half-time); Eoghan O'Gara for McCarthy (61 mins); Eamon Fennell for Bastick (65 mins); Ross McConnell for Flynn (67 mins)

DONEGAL: Paul Durcan; Karl Lacey, Eamon McGee, Niall McGee; Kevin Cassidy (0-1), Paddy McGrath, Anthony Thompson; Rory Kavanagh, Ryan Bradley (0-1); Mark McHugh, Michael Murphy, Christy Toye; Colm McFadden (0-4, 0-2 frees), David Walsh, Frank McGlynn. Subs: Michael Hegarty for Toye (half-time); Marty Boyle for Lacey (42 mins); Martin McElhinney for Hegarty (64 mins); Paddy McBrearty for Boyle (67 mins)

Referee: Maurice Deegan (Laois)

CHAPTEREIGHT
JUDGEMENT DAY

In the weeks running up to the All Ireland final, it gradually became clear that the rivalry between Dublin and Kerry wasn't what it used to be.

'It has a resonance for the fans, but not so much for the players,' said Kerry manager Jack O'Connor in *The Irish Times* a few days before the final. 'When this rivalry was taking off in the mid 1970s most of these players weren't even born. In '75 I was only 15 years myself, but for the players they'd only know it through videos and the rest so it wouldn't have the same resonance, but the older fans have a great grá for Dublin–Kerry, no doubt.'

So although there was a small element of wheeling out the former greats in the papers and on the TV – 'the geriatrics', Mikey Sheehy called them – it was done with half a heart. The stories had all been told and retold a thousand times and more. As 1970s Dublin legend Anton O'Toole put it in an *Irish Examiner* interview, 'Nowadays if you want someone to tell you how great you were, find a Kerry fella you played against and you can pat each other on the back and we can say weren't we wonderful.'

Instead, the first week after Dublin's semi-final was dominated by talk of neither Dublin nor Kerry but Donegal. There had been wholly predictable uproar over the semi-final, and Jim McGuinness found himself held up as the embodiment of all that is wrong with the game. It was distinctly unfair on McGuinness, who was a brilliant young coach who'd spent the majority of his playing career on Donegal teams that were as flaky as just-grilled fish. Far from being lauded for the strides Donegal had made in his first year, he was having to listen to TV pundits tell the world that his players wouldn't have enjoyed playing for their county this year.

For Pat Gilroy, a week of *Sturm und Drang* about another county who weren't even in the final was perfect. He had three weeks to prepare

his team for the final, and the more of it that the outside world could waste on things he didn't have to get involved in the better.

Gilroy had his plan for the three weeks worked out and ready to go. The day after the semi-final, each player was given an itinerary of what the three weeks would hold for them. As John Fogarty later wrote in the *Irish Examiner*, they were told who would be going to the press day the following Friday, where and when each training session would be, everything.

A veteran of lost All Ireland finals himself back in the day, Gilroy wanted to remove from the equation any small thing that could possibly allow players to get ahead of themselves. Ten days before the game, the GPA were holding an event to publicize the fact that they were joining their All Star scheme up with the traditional one, so that instead of there being two teams of the year in hurling and football, there would now be one in each code. They thought they had lined up a Dublin player and a Kerry player to attend the launch, but the Dublin management had other ideas.

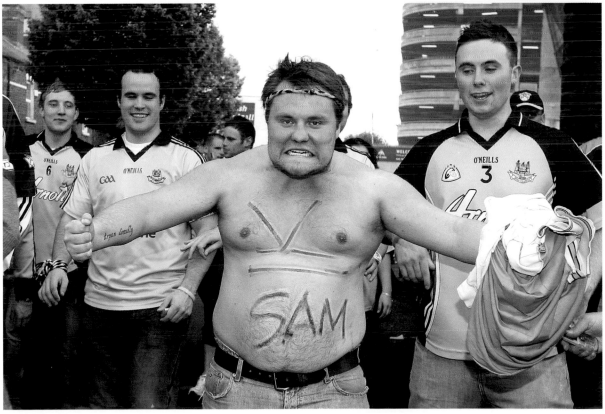

Gilroy wanted to remove from the equation any small thing that could possibly allow players to get ahead of themselves.

It was a familiar theme in the build-up, as Alan Brogan would explain after the final. 'There was a bit of stuff not just for myself, there were a number of fellas who sacrificed stuff,' he told the *Examiner*. 'At the end of the day, winning a football match is a lot bigger than any of that stuff and it helped to galvanize the team …We just decided it was about winning a football match and that was it.'

It was old-fashioned and it probably cost his players a few of the scarce money-making opportunities their standing in the game afforded them, but in the end, the team and the squad came first.

The days of the 6.30 a.m. training sessions were long gone. And in the run-up to the final, there weren't a huge number of 7.30 p.m. ones either. The last thing Gilroy wanted was a repeat of 1995, when hordes had descended on Dublin's training sessions. They held training sessions at 3.30 in the afternoon. Invariably, that meant they held them without an audience.

Gilroy got in contact with former panel member Conal Keaney, who was the sales manager at the Avon Rí resort in Blessington, Co. Wicklow, to see if he could organize accommodation for the squad at short notice. He could, and the whole panel decamped there for the weekend of the All Ireland hurling final. There was pitch for them to train on and meeting rooms for them to hatch plans in. It got them out of the city and into the groove.

The day before the final, they were put through one final training session. The warm-up on All Ireland final day was to be shorter than usual because of pre-match formalities, so they replicated the shorter warm-up in the final training session. As Brogan would tell John Fogarty later, they even had a mock red-carpet drill.

Always when an All Ireland is won, little details like this emerge and take on disproportionate significance. In reality, they barely mattered. You fill time as best you can in the lead-up to an All Ireland, and standing players in a line to meet a fake president killed 10 minutes and got them laughing. There wouldn't be much time for that the following day.

They even had a mock red-carpet drill.

The sign reads: "THE BROGANS HAVE SWAGGER AND CLUXTON MOVES LIKE JAGGER"

OPPOSITE
Stephen Cluxton
punches a high
ball away from
Kieran O'Leary.

After a brutal night's rain, the day dawned grey around Croke Park. Crowds started to gather around the Ballybough pubs from just after 10.30 in the morning. Grand old Dublin hideouts like Gaffney's and Meagher's that had had to put up with years of wall-to-wall culchies on All Ireland final day were populated with their own from early on. Nervy locals reading the papers and then reading them again but still not being able to tell you what they said. Fathers and sons and grandfathers trying to knock fun out of a morning that wasn't fun. Loudmouths telling the same old jokes with a bravado the rest of them couldn't muster.

Grand old Dublin hideouts like Gaffney's and Meagher's that had had to put up with years of wall-to-wall culchies on All Ireland final day were populated with their own from early on.

Up to the stadium for the minor game. The young Dubs were caught at the death by a heroic Tipperary side who'd made a habit of coming back from huge deficits all summer. As a tiny band of Tipp supporters high in the Upper Cusack sang 'Slievenamon', Dublin hearts were heavy. Earlier in the summer, Dublin's minor and under-21 hurlers had lost All Ireland finals; if the senior footballers didn't win now, it would mean four All Ireland final defeats in the one year for the county. Regardless of the strides made in both football and hurling, that would be a tough one to take.

Both sides picked the same 15 that had started the semi-finals. Diarmuid Connolly had been sent off against Donegal, but Dublin had got his ban overturned very early on and it never became a saga that might take energy from their preparations.

Of more concern was the hamstring injury to Paul Flynn; it was touch and go right up until the day as to whether he'd start or not. Two things made up the selectors' minds for them: for one, Flynn just about passed a fitness test the day before the game; for another, Gilroy was keen to keep Kevin McManamon back as an impact sub. He'd made a difference in every game he'd come off the bench for, most especially against Wexford and Donegal. He had a knack for spotting gaps and knowing whose shoulder to run at as defenders tired. If Gilroy could keep him back and get 45 minutes out of Flynn, he would.

In Kerry, Jack O'Connor had no massive injury worries, but what he did have was an extremely fit, extremely enthusiastic Paul Galvin pushing for a place in the first 15. Between injury and suspension and one thing and another, Galvin had gone a full two years without playing a full 70 minutes for Kerry. His campaign this summer had been limited to a few excursions off the bench, but he'd made a very noticeable impact on the semi-final against Mayo. He'd been dynamic and fleet-footed, bouncing in and out of traffic like the man who won Footballer of the Year in 2009.

Jack O'Connor had no massive injury worries, but what he did have was an extremely fit, extremely enthusiastic Paul Galvin.

OPPOSITE
Kerry achieved early supremacy in the battle to control kick-outs; here, Denis Bastick and Barry Cahill compete with Bryan Sheehan and Aidan O'Mahony.

NEXT SPREAD
Declan O'Sullivan goes to ground under the attentions of Ger Brennan.

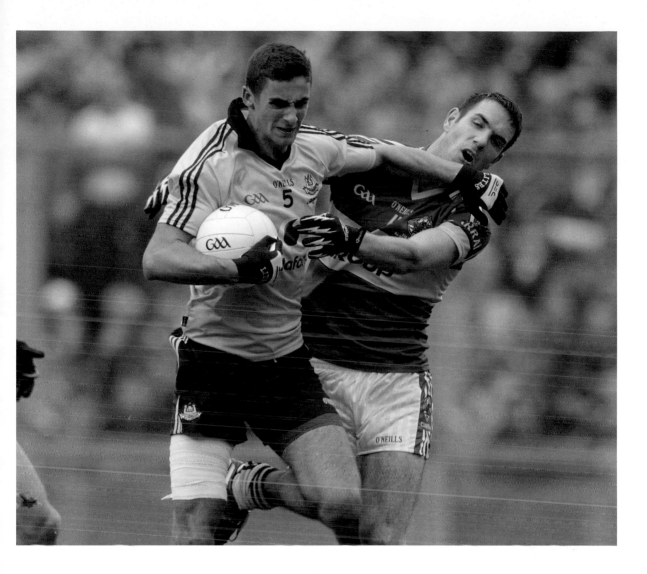

In the end, though, O'Connor chose to leave him on the subs bench. Partly, this may have been down to the fact that the man whose place he would have taken was likely to be Donnchadh Walsh – the least flashy of the Kerry forwards and a man who had played every game up to the final before losing his place in 2009. To do it to him once was a tough call; to have done it to him twice would have been bordering on cruel. Walsh was a fine, honest player who hadn't done a whole lot wrong. The other consideration was that when O'Connor looked at the Kerry bench, he didn't see a huge amount of depth. Just like McManamon with the Dubs, Galvin would be a very useful arrow to have in the quiver.

O'Connor had one big trick up his sleeve. Kieran Donaghy went out to midfield for the throw-in as he had done for all of Kerry's matches through the summer. But instead of loping back in towards full-forward, he stationed himself at wing-forward for the opening stages. And as the game shook itself awake, he was the dominant figure. He hung back for

Kerry kick-outs and pushed forward for Dublin's, ran over and back the width of the pitch and caused all sorts of havoc. In all the scenarios the Dublin management had drawn up, Donaghy as a roving trouble-maker hadn't arisen.

Kerry had spent the whole of the first half against Mayo lashing long high balls into the full-forward line, but they were being more nuanced here and it was allowing them the better start. Declan O'Sullivan fisted the first point of the day after a strong Darran O'Sullivan run. But for all that Kerry were making the better opening, they weren't making it count on the scoreboard, and when Dublin pounced on a couple of Kerry errors for points by Alan Brogan in the 11th and 15th minutes, Dublin were ahead.

Coming up on 19 minutes on the clock, Darran O'Sullivan zipped through the Dublin defence before feeding Colm Cooper on the 20-metre line. Cooper collected, feinted and shot in one movement, placing a sonnet of a finish beyond Stephen Cluxton and into the left corner of the net.

In all the scenarios the Dublin management had drawn up, Donaghy as a roving trouble-maker hadn't arisen.

OPPOSITE
Darran O'Sullivan's pace gave the Dublin defence trouble throughout the first half.

ABOVE
Barry Cahill and Bryan Cullen double-team Killian Young.

JUDGEMENT DAY

CHAPTER EIGHT

PREVIOUS SPREAD
Colm Cooper
celebrates his goal.

OPPOSITE TOP
An off-the-ball
incident between
Rory O'Carroll and
Declan O'Sullivan
drew Kerry manager
Jack O'Connor
onto the pitch.

OPPOSITE BOTTOM
The introduction of
Paul Galvin with ten
minutes to go in the
first half was a bold
move, but Galvin
struggled to make
an impact.

It was a stunning goal. O'Sullivan's run had almost left scorch-marks in the turf as he drew the Dublin defence towards him yet always stayed out of their reach. The sheer terror he'd created had made a yard of space for Cooper. You didn't have to be watching the sport for very long before you understood what a yard of space 20 metres from goal meant to Colm Cooper. It meant an umpire walking forward and picking up a green flag, more often than not. Kerry 1–1, Dublin 0–2. Game on.

Almost immediately, O'Connor decided it was time to spring Galvin from the bench, in place of Kieran O'Leary. It seemed an odd decision. True, Kerry only had two scores to show for the first 20 minutes, but by bringing Galvin on they would be playing their strongest bench card very early – and sending Donaghy into the full-forward line. The thinking was presumably that Donaghy was having such a good day that getting him on the ball closer to goal should bring better results.

As it turned out, the opposite happened. With Donaghy gone from centrefield, Dublin got a foothold there. In his eagerness to get into the game, Galvin committed a few fouls. When Bernard Brogan and Cluxton converted, Dublin were level; and when Brogan scored an excellent point of his own from out on the left on 29 minutes, they were ahead and in the driving seat.

Kerry hadn't scored since Cooper's goal and had completely lost their way around the middle of the pitch. Another Brogan free on 32 minutes put Dublin two points ahead, and it took an important intercession from Galvin to send Kerry into the break with a spot of relief. Latching on to a clever Cooper pass a minute before half–time, he popped a point to leave the margin at just one. Dublin 0–6, Kerry 1–2.

It was an arm-wrestle of a game. Nine scores in the first half was only three better than Dublin and Donegal had managed in the second half of their notorious semi-final. But this was different. This wasn't a stalemate, more of a feeling-out phase. Every pass mattered and every move mattered, but there was no doubt that defences were on top. And in a game like that, Dublin had a shot.

Actually, they had more than a shot. If it was anybody else, you'd have said they were favourites from that point on. They'd survived Kerry's tactical masterstroke, forced them to abandon it even. If it was anybody else, you'd have favoured the younger team playing the better football with the more potent reserves yet to join the fray. But this was Dublin and we'd been here before and it hadn't been pretty. They had 35 minutes to banish those days for good.

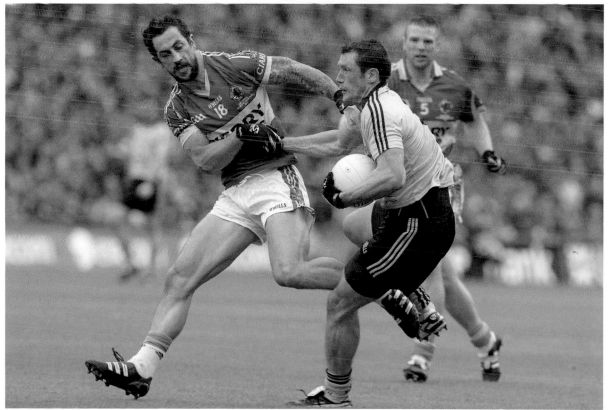

THE PROMISED LAND

Did Dublin believe? They certainly came out and began the second half as though they did. The first half had gone reasonably well, but in the dressing room at the break, some of Ray Boyne's statistics wouldn't have made for the most encouraging reading. Kerry had done their homework on Stephen Cluxton's kick-outs – the source of so much that was good about Dublin's year – and were winning lots of balls from them. In Dublin's system, responsibility for kick-outs did not fall solely to the midfielders, but Denis Bastick and Michael Darragh Macauley would have felt a need to respond.

Two minutes in, Barry Cahill flicked a short handpass to midfield partner Macauley, who took off on a run. He laid it off to Bryan Cullen but kept running, drawing two Kerry defenders over towards him. Cullen fed Alan Brogan, who had seen Macauley's run and processed the ball as quickly as he could, leaving the big midfielder with Bryan Sheehan and Marc Ó Sé between him and the goal.

He fixed on a gap between them and burst at it, not unlike the way Ireland flanker Seán O'Brien had done against Australia in a famous Rugby World Cup victory the previous day. In the end, he had to be dragged down from behind by Sheehan with a desperate pull of the jersey – making a mockery of Jack O'Connor's claim that such cynicism wasn't in the DNA of Kerry footballers. As Macauley went back to his position, Bernard Brogan met him with a defiant high-five. Point made.

From the kick-out, Dublin bumped and ground out the dirty ball. Cullen got on it twice, Kevin Nolan a couple of times as well. When Cullen looked like he might be bottled up, it was Bastick who made the space out on the left. He drove at the Kerry defence, not unlike his midfield partner had done just a minute beforehand. A quick exchange

OPPOSITE TOP
**Mick Fitzsimons
ushers the ball to
safety with Colm
Cooper lurking.**

OPPOSITE BOTTOM
**Tom O'Sullivan
expresses his
frustration.**

of passes with Bernard Brogan left him clear in front of goal and he hoisted one over the bar. Point made.

A minute later, Declan O'Sullivan kicked a hurried wide into the Canal End. Kerry were three points down and were looking sluggish in comparison to the Dubs. The clock had just turned 40 minutes and we really hadn't seen very much from them since Colm Cooper's goal on 19 minutes. Three points down against a younger team who had just begun the second half correcting the one area that had ailed them in the first half. If Kerry were inclined to panic, now would have been the time to start.

But that's not really who they are. And they knew that as long as they were still able to pressure the Dublin kick-out, they were in with a shout. From O'Sullivan's wide, Kerry hustled Cahill off the ball and set up a move that ended with Sheehan pointing a free. From the next one, Anthony Maher caught cleanly and fed Tomás Ó Sé, and his high diagonal ball into Kieran Donaghy – by now on the edge of the square again – was inch-perfect. Donaghy caught the ball above Rory O'Carroll's head and fisted over the bar.

Had he held it a split second longer he might have been able to put Darran O'Sullivan in for a goal, but the catch and score was pure adrenalin. Kerry were stirring and when they won the next kick-out as well, Dublin were suddenly in real trouble. Declan O'Sullivan surged into the Dublin defence only to be met with the stiffest of forearms from Ger Brennan, who was lucky that Joe McQuillan only flashed a yellow card his way.

Cooper pointed the free and just like that Kerry were level. After taking the whole of the first half to raise two white flags, Kerry had now added three points in two and a half minutes and had wiped out the lead Dublin had so painstakingly built. All on their dominance of the Dublin kick-out.

If Kerry were inclined to panic, now would have been the time to start.

Pat Gilroy needed to change things. The area around their half-backs and half-forwards was being cleaned out.

Pat Gilroy needed to change things. The area around their half-backs and half-forwards was being cleaned out. James McCarthy and Paul Flynn were both heavily strapped in the leg, and the decision was taken not to make them carry the fight any longer. McCarthy made way for Philly McMahon. Four minutes later, Flynn was replaced by Kevin McManamon.

By now, Kerry had gone a point ahead through Sheehan. His point was the sort of score you began to feel would see Kerry home. Barry Cahill had run into traffic on the Kerry 45 and been forced to give away a free for over-carrying. Aidan O'Mahony had taken a quick free and Kerry were moving – through Declan O'Sullivan and Anthony Maher and then Sheehan. All very patient, all very precise, it looked like the mark of a team of champions finding its feet.

Bernard Brogan tapped over a free that should never have been given to draw the sides level again, but Kerry didn't fret. Sheehan kicked a 45 and then a free, Cooper kicked one of his own. On RTÉ's television commentary, Ger Canning started to count chickens. 'A goal and two for Cooper,' he said, 'and Kerry fans are already contemplating taking Sam Maguire home to Killarney tomorrow night.'

McManamon was finding it hard to insinuate his way into the game and lost the ball too often to make a difference. Eoghan O'Gara came on for Cahill, Eamon Fennell for Bastick. All the changes were around the middle, where the fight for possession was the fight for the All Ireland.

When Anthony Maher won yet another kick-out on 63 minutes and fed Cooper for yet another point, we were beyond the point of counting chickens. This was over. The All Ireland final now was about Cooper, the footballer of his generation and one of the most cherished Kerry players of all time, getting to lift the Sam Maguire as captain. This was his eighth All Ireland final and apart from his first one against Armagh in 2002 – when he was only 19 – he had been Kerry's leading scorer in every one of those games. It was an incredible record, the mark of a uniquely gifted player.

Did Kerry believe they had it won? Did Dublin? You'd have forgiven either side for entertaining the thought just then. Kerry's dominance of the Dublin kick-out continued, Paul Galvin tidying up the loose ball Cluxton had sent out to the left wing. But from here, they got sloppy. Inexplicably so. As Cluxton had been readying the kick-out, Daniel Bohan came on for Eoin Brosnan, but instead of funnelling back to block up the centre-back area he joined in the play as Galvin fed him. After he dished off a pass to Maher, he went forward to see if the move had promise. Kerry were short one defender now.

Killian Young went to collect the ball in midfield, leaving a tired Alan Brogan trailing in his wake. Afterwards, the finger would be pointed at Declan O'Sullivan, but actually the point at which this All Ireland final changed for good was when Young failed to collect a simple ball from O'Sullivan when he had 15 yards of space around him. Under no pressure, he spilled the ball and by the time he collected it, the option of a quick pass forward to Bohan was gone. Bohan had nobody on him and Darran O'Sullivan free to his right on the Dublin 45; a pass to either would have given Kerry the chance to close the game out for good. Instead, having fumbled, Young went backwards and fed Declan O'Sullivan inside. By now, Alan Brogan had hustled back and was able to get a hand in the air as O'Sullivan tried to find the onrushing Aidan O'Mahony – yet another Kerry defender looking to get forward. When Cian O'Sullivan managed to get to the breaking ball, O'Mahony and Young converged upon him.

Kerry were in huge trouble but it seemed that only Declan O'Sullivan realized it. He saw that not only was Bohan stranded upfield now but Young and O'Mahony were stuck in midfield, so he sprinted back towards his full-back line. Had Young and O'Mahony at least rugby tackled Cian O'Sullivan to the ground, Kerry might have bought an extra few seconds and survived. As it was, he was able to play a quick free to Alan Brogan and Dublin were away.

With no O'Mahony, no Young and no Bohan, Brogan and McManamon had the whole of the Cusack Stand side of the Kerry half to themselves. Once McManamon latched onto Brogan's quick

Kerry were in huge trouble but it seemed that only Declan O'Sullivan realized it.

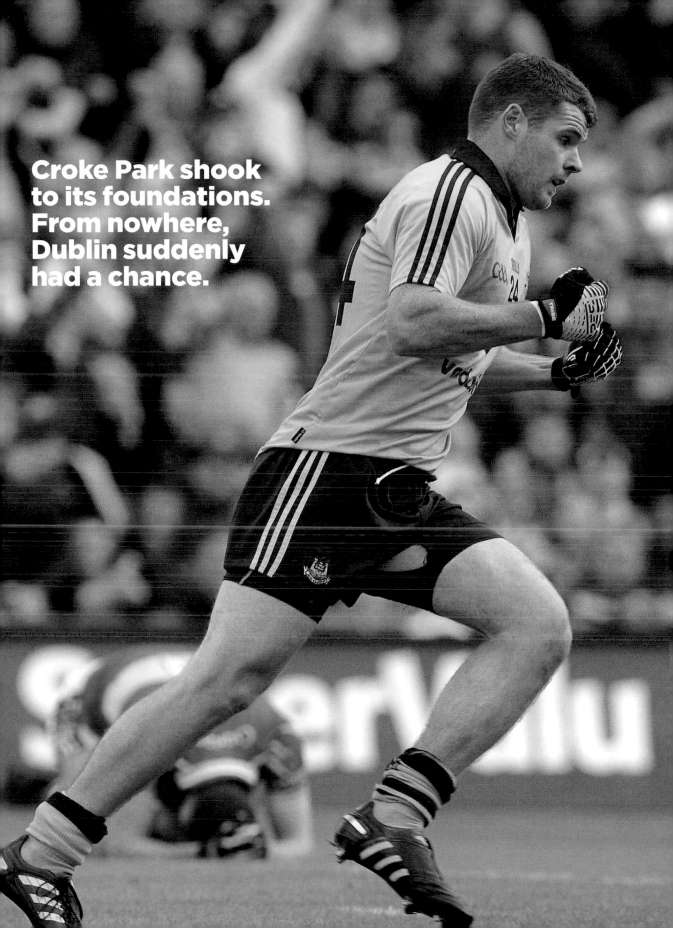

**Croke Park shook
to its foundations.
From nowhere,
Dublin suddenly
had a chance.**

PREVIOUS SPREAD
Kevin McManamon's
goal turned the final
on its head.

pass, the only body he had in front of him was the retreating Declan O'Sullivan. Going at pace, his sidestep was always going to win out and his low finish gave Brendan Kealy no chance. Goal. Game back on.

Croke Park shook to its foundations. From nowhere, Dublin suddenly had a chance. And when Tom O'Sullivan gave away a loose handpass in midfield 40 seconds later, Dublin were able to pick out Kevin Nolan wandering free outside the Kerry 45. Despite never having scored a point for Dublin in his life, Nolan decided to try one from distance. When you're on a roll, you're on a roll. The sides were level, Kerry's lead rubbed out inside the space of a minute.

Everybody needed a breather. Bernard Brogan went down to have some cramp attended to. Kerry tried to slow everything down, to keep possession and maybe work a score. They tried one pass too many, albeit they might have had a free when Cooper was fouled in the left corner. Dublin turned the ball over but almost gave it back straight away as McManamon hopped the ball twice, right on his own 45. Joe McQuillan didn't notice the transgression. Afterwards, Kerry would make it clear they weren't going to give out about the referee in a way that left you in no doubt that they would do plenty of it when they were amongst themselves.

With two minutes to go, Dublin got a line-ball when a hasty fly-hack from Kealy beat Young and went out over the sideline. Alan Brogan kicked it infield to Diarmuid Connolly, who had been quiet in the final so far. Indeed, he'd been quiet since the Tyrone game, as Donegal had frustrated the last nerve out of him in the semi-final. If ever there was a chance to shrug off the slightly flaky reputation he'd garnered for himself, now was the time.

Connolly burst onto Brogan's pass and found that he had first Donaghy for company and then Bohan into the bargain. Buffeted by both, he held on to possession long enough for Macauley to run past him. Connolly's pass inside opened up space ahead of the Dublin midfielder, who waited for Bernard Brogan to loop out behind him before laying it off. Dublin's top scorer did the necessary and put them ahead. Going from four points down to a point up had taken just over four minutes.

Going from four points down to a point up had taken just over four minutes.

They could have gone two up but Macauley blazed wide in the next attack. Kealy took a short kick-out to Young, who looked across the full-back line and went to pick out Marc Ó Sé in the space under the Hogan Stand. As soon as it left his boot, Young threw both hands to his head in horror. The kick was far too high and would have looked too long from where he was standing. Not only that, it was a good five yards behind Ó Sé when Kerry needed to be heading in the direction of the Canal End.

Ó Sé didn't blink. Like Cooper, this was his eighth All Ireland final and he'd had a good day so far. He ran back and caught the ball above his head, coming down just inside the sideline. As he did so, the clock on the two big screens inside the ground turned 69.00.

He swung around to face the Dublin goal. Pat Gilroy was standing no more than two yards away, frantically waving O'Gara and Brogan back up the pitch. O'Gara had been in the game for just 11 minutes at this point and he sprinted back with all he had; Brogan had run his legs to stumps and was bent over with his hands on his knees but still he broke into one last jog. Giving all he had as well.

Ó Sé made ground quickly around a very tired Cullen. He dished off to his brother Tomás, who was about four yards inside the sideline at midfield and who realized that there were eight Dublin players either patrolling the right flank of the pitch or on their way there. Kerry needed to switch the play to work an escape route.

The elder Ó Sé fisted the ball back inside to Galvin, who instantly fed it further infield to Sheehan. The Kerry number 9 crossed the halfway mark with a solo and as his loping stride took him across the Dublin 65-metre line, he launched a fist-pass over towards the Cusack Stand sideline, where Maher collected right on the 45. Kerry were moving now. Dublin couldn't get a hand in anywhere. The effort they'd put in to grab the game back was showing.

Just as Maher collected, Kieran Donaghy came sprinting out from in front of the goal and headed for the sideline. Maher laid it off to the onrushing Bohan, who had made a 60-yard run to get involved. Bohan had actually been closer to the Hill than Galvin when Galvin had passed to Sheehan seven seconds earlier and now he was carrying the ball right up to the Dublin 21-metre line. His defensive duties didn't matter anymore, not with Kerry in need of a score.

Donaghy lost Cian O'Sullivan, looped out around Bohan and demanded a pass. He caught Bohan's flick with one eye on the posts and launched the ball into the clouds. It took an age to come down, but by the time it did, Cluxton was hanging from the crossbar. The sides were

OPPOSITE
With seconds to go,
Kevin McManamon
wins a free from
Barry John Keane.

level. Kerry supporters in the ground breathed out. Their team had gone the length of the pitch without a Dublin player being able to lay a finger on a man in possession. The move had taken 35 seconds and had gone through nine pairs of Kerry hands, using the full width and length of Croke Park. In the circumstances, it was an extraordinary score.

As Cluxton put down the ball for the kick-out, the PA announced that there would be two minutes of additional time. The final hadn't seen a replay since 2000. 'These teams have been level six times here in Croke Park,' said Darragh Maloney, commentating for RTÉ Radio. 'We would love to see them do it all again.'

Both teams had other ideas. As Cluxton kicked the ball out, the clock said 69:52. Ger Brennan pounced on the loose ball from the kick-out and drew a free. Donaghy, who'd been fired up all game and had been making a nuisance of himself at every turn, tried to prevent him from taking a quick one. Brennan pushed a hand into the Kerry forward's face, sending him to the ground. The referee whistled. Throw ball.

Donaghy went in for it with Eamon Fennell. The same Fennell who'd spent two years trying to fight the system, the same Fennell who had been through more to get to play in a Dublin jersey than most players would have had the stomach for. He and Donaghy jostled for it and Fennell got the most important fingertip of his life to the ball. Alan Brogan cleaned up and fed McManamon. The clock said 70:29.

On Dublin pushed. McManamon to Cullen. Cullen to Macauley. Macauley to Connolly. Again, Connolly was stronger in possession than popular wisdom would have expected. Again, he held up the ball and waited for support to arrive. Again, he made a difference in a way not many people would have thought he could.

And then the pass inside. The reach from McManamon. The jink from left to right that threw Barry John Keane. McManamon hitting the turf. Joe McQuillan calling a foul.

Time stood still. Bernard Brogan took the ball from McManamon and patted him on the back, then turned to the Canal End again to wave Cluxton forward. The walk-up took a whole minute. Coolest man in the place.

Five steps back. Two to the left. Ten seconds left on the clock. A rub of the gloves on the front of his shirt. A punch of left glove into the right. A run-up. A plant of the right foot. A swing of the left.

Straight between the posts.

ALL IRELAND SFC FINAL
CROKE PARK, 18 SEPTEMBER 2011
DUBLIN 1–12, KERRY 1–11

DUBLIN: Stephen Cluxton (0-2, frees); Mick Fitzsimons, Rory O'Carroll, Cian O'Sullivan; James McCarthy, Ger Brennan, Kevin Nolan (0-1); Michael Darragh Macauley, Denis Bastick (0-1); Paul Flynn, Barry Cahill, Bryan Cullen; Alan Brogan (0-2), Diarmuid Connolly, Bernard Brogan (0-6, 0-4 frees). Subs: Philly McMahon for McCarthy (46 mins); Kevin McManamon (1-0) for Flynn (51 mins); Eoghan O'Gara for Cahill (57 mins); Eamon Fennell for Bastick (63 mins)

KERRY: Brendan Kealy; Marc Ó Sé, Tom O'Sullivan, Killian Young; Tomás Ó Sé, Aidan O'Mahony, Eoin Brosnan; Anthony Maher, Bryan Sheehan (0-4, 0-2 frees, 0-1 45); Donnchadh Walsh, Darran O'Sullivan, Kieran Donaghy (0-2); Colm Cooper (1-3, 0-2 frees), Declan O'Sullivan (0-1), Kieran O'Leary. Subs: Paul Galvin (0-1) for O'Leary (24 mins); Barry John Keane for Walsh (51 mins); Daniel Bohan for Brosnan (63 mins)

Referee: Joe McQuillan (Cavan)

BLUE
HEAVEN

You just run. What else is there to do? The whistle goes, long, long and long. And then that's it. All the years and tears and fears are gone. Every row is brushed away, every jibe and jeer locked up in a box.

So they just ran. To the nearest blue shirt. To the nearest drawn face suddenly cracked open wide. Alan Brogan ran to Bryan Cullen and Eamon Fennell. Ger Brennan ran to jump on top of the three of them. Mick Fitzsimons came 20 yards to join the pile. Eoghan O'Gara thought about running but first sank to his knees. Michael Darragh Macauley went straight to the ground, as though he hadn't another step in him. Stephen Cluxton was still running back from taking the free and he jumped and punched the air. Rory O'Carroll ran in to join him in the goal.

Pat Gilroy ran for a couple of steps, then turned and balled his fists and roared. It had been largely overlooked throughout the build-up but Joe McQuillan's final whistle technically ended Gilroy's reign as Dublin manager. He'd signed up for three terms and three terms were done now. Whatever he did now, he was a made man. All Ireland winner as player and manager.

Mickey Whelan ran past him. His substitutes bench emptied and ran out past him too. Little flash-fires of Dublin players erupted around the pitch before gradually, inexorably, they were drawn to the one place they knew they had to run. Nobody said it, nobody ordered it – but they all knew where they were going. So they ran, en masse, to Hill 16.

Nobody said it, nobody ordered it – but they all knew where they were going. So they ran, en masse, to Hill 16.

OPPOSITE
Bryan Cullen, the first
Dublin captain to lift
the Sam Maguire Cup
in 16 years.

The bookies had laid odds on whether there'd be a pitch invasion. After 16 years, nothing would test Croke Park's attempts to keep people off the pitch like a Dublin All Ireland. But it had all held up – the fence and the stewards had done their job. So running to the Hill was the least the players could do.

After that, the day was snapshots. Cullen lifting Sam and rounding off his speech by inviting the whole city to join them in Copper Face Jacks. O'Gara getting the bumps to celebrate having become a father and an All Ireland winner in the same weekend. The players coming across Pillar Caffrey during their lap of honour as he was on duty as a Garda and greeting him with genuine warmth and affection.

Gilroy handing out hugs to every last player and physio and statsman. Andy Kettle bouncing around the place like a young lad. Mossy Quinn, David Henry and Paul Casey drinking it all in, having come through hell to make it to this point. They'd got their All Ireland now and let nobody say they hadn't earned it just because they didn't play this time around. They'd played enough.

Kerry's grace in defeat. Tomás Ó Sé summoning up as noble a gesture as the old place has seen by collecting the ball Cluxton had kicked over the bar and walking the length of the pitch to hand it to the Dublin goalkeeper. Marc Ó Sé saying that Bernard and Alan Brogan were 'too good not to have All Ireland medals'. A broken Kieran Donaghy, speaking in a near-whisper, saying: 'It's a hard one to take but that's life. There are people in hospitals all over the country now who are worse off than we are right at this moment.'

When Gilroy reflected on it all afterwards, he took time to think of the people who had been there a lot longer than him. You didn't have to know a lot about the Dublin story to see that it was about more than one year. Most counties are lucky enough not to get slapped about in front of the whole country every year, fortunate to be able to slink out of the championship without anyone really noticing. That option is never open to the Dubs. If you're a Dublin footballer, every championship exit is like your date throwing a glass of wine over you in a crowded restaurant. Gilroy knew there were plenty of people who deserved better.

You didn't have to know a lot about the Dublin story to see that it was about more than one year.

'There's only so much pain humans can take,' he said. 'I mean I've only been here a short time really in comparison to some of these fellas. But as a supporter we've been through terrible days here and there's only so much of that you can keep taking. Today, no matter what happened, we're going to get the result to be honest. That's the attitude we had all week. We weren't just happy getting to a final. We wanted to push on, and win it.'

'You couldn't write it in a fairytale,' said Bernard Brogan. 'I'm just thrilled and I'm delighted that my da has a bit of bragging rights now when we go down to Kerry. We spent our time growing up in Listowel and listening to them talk about All Irelands but in fairness to them they've always had a good word to say about Dublin and they have always respected us.

'I'm just delighted that we have something we can challenge them with. I never thought I'd be here, after beating Kerry in an All Ireland final. I'm just delighted for Alan, who has given 10 years of trojan work, and he must be in line for footballer of the year. Last year, me and Pat had a chat when I won player of the year and he was saying, "Congratulations, delighted," but we have to get back to square one and he said, "My dream is that we win an All Ireland against Kerry next year and Alan is player of the year." So we're nearly there.'

OPPOSITE TOP
Kevin Nolan, who was later named man of the match.

OPPOSITE BOTTOM
Paul Flynn hails Hill 16 with the cup.

ABOVE
Paul Casey with Alan Brogan and Alan's little boy Jamie.

Typically, the man who kicked the winning score was nowhere to be found. Cluxton had stayed on the pitch to watch Cullen lift the trophy, but as soon as his speech was over, the Dublin goalkeeper had walked down the tunnel alongside the Kerry players. It was his right as much as anyone's to take his place on the podium and lift the most famous trophy in Irish sport above his head but he declined. Even though his team called after him, he waved them away.

The Sunday papers the following week carried the remarkable tale of how RTÉ reporter Marty Morrissey had seen Cluxton slope off and followed him into the dressing room. 'Will you not come out for the presentation, Stephen?' he asked. 'Ah no,' said Cluxton. 'I'll leave them at it.' For that half-hour, Cluxton was probably the most famous man in Ireland but he didn't want a bit of it. Just as when Ó Sé had handed him the match ball, he'd appreciated the gesture but had still kicked the ball gently away. He didn't want fame, he didn't want souvenirs. He just wanted to win.

OPPOSITE
Eoghan O'Gara celebrates the All Ireland – and becoming a father.

ABOVE
Pat Gilroy shares a laugh with Denis Bastick.

Typically, the man who kicked the winning score was nowhere to be found.

The aftermath went on for days. That night at the banquet, Kevin Nolan was the RTÉ choice for man of the match. It had been some year for the 22-year-old. A county championship with Kilmacud, an All Ireland with Dublin and now this. He'd even met the Queen when she'd visited Croke Park. She'd shaken hands with four current inter-county players that day, but Nolan was the only one ending the year with an All Ireland medal.

Sunday bled into Monday without many players seeing their beds. A handful went on the traditional visit to the children's hospitals the next day, sprinkling a little hope and light into kids fighting tougher battles than they could know. The panel got the afternoon off from official duties and spread out through the city.

By the evening they were back together again, this time on a stage in Merrion Square where an estimated 40,000 people turned up to receive them. One by one, they held the cup aloft for the crowd, soaking up the experience.

As the days passed and life started regaining some sort of balance, it was easy to imagine that the experience might be repeated soon. This was a young Dublin team, all in all. Denis Bastick and Barry Cahill were the only 30-year-olds in the starting line-up, with Alan Brogan and Stephen Cluxton at 29. None of them was making noises about going

anywhere. And though the minors had thrown their final away against Tipperary, nobody doubted that there was some electrifying talent coming up through the ranks. It seemed certain, for instance, that Ciarán Kilkenny would be in the senior squad before long and that more would follow him.

But those were worries for another day. By the end of the week, Gilroy, Cullen and the two Brogans were dressed up in their official suits again and doing *The Late Late Show*. A long winter of engagements lay ahead, answering the same questions and talking through the same stories. They'd been to clubs and schools and colleges already during the week and they'd be to many more in time. Whenever it became too wearisome, any time they flagged, they'd just remind themselves that the alternative would have been far worse.

Dublin football had spent enough time with its head down, looking at the ground. Now it was time to face the sun.

OPPOSITE
The brothers Brogan – Bernard, Paul and Alan – celebrate with Sam.

ABOVE
The players take their own photos in the warm-up room.

KEVIN MCMANAMON

EAMON FENNELL